D1480738

Reading and Interpreting the Works of

J. R. R. TOLKIEN

Enslow Publishing
101 W. 23rd Street
Suite 240
New York, NY 10011
USA
enslow.com

Lit Crit
Guides

Reading and Interpreting
the Works of

J. R. R.
TOLKIEN

Greg Clinton

Published in 2017 by Enslow Publishing, LLC
101 W. 23rd Street, Suite 240, New York, NY 10011

Library of Congress Cataloging-in-Publication Data

Names: Clinton, Greg, author.
Title: Reading and interpreting the works of J.R.R. Tolkien / Greg Clinton.
Description: New York, NY : Enslow Publishing, 2017. | Series: Lit crit guides | Includes bibliographical references and index.
Identifiers: LCCN 2016026259 | ISBN 9780766083622 (library bound)
Subjects: LCSH: Tolkien, J. R. R. (John Ronald Reuel), 1892-1973—Criticism and interpretation—Juvenile literature.
Classification: LCC PR6039.O32 Z62244 2016 | DDC 828/.91209—dc23
LC record available at https://lccn.loc.gov/2016026259

Printed in Malaysia

To Our Readers: We have done our best to make sure all website addresses in this book were active and appropriate when we went to press. However, the author and the publisher have no control over and assume no liability for the material available on those websites or on any websites they may link to. Any comments or suggestions can be sent by e-mail to customerservice@enslow.com.

Photo Credits: Cover, pp. 3, 57 Time Life Pictures/The LIFE Images Collection/Getty Images; p. 6 © AP Images; p. 8 Paul Popper/Popperfoto/Getty Images; pp. 12, 48 © Pamela Chandler/ArenaPal/The Image Works; pp. 17, 92 Private Collection/Bridgeman Images; p. 19 Heritage Images/Hulton Fine Art Collection/Getty Images; p. 21 Wolf Suschitzky/The LIFE Images Collection/Getty Images; p. 23 Universal History Archive/Universal Images Group/Getty Images; p. 28 ullstein bild/Getty Images; p. 35 Rick Eglinton/Toronto Star/Getty Images; p. 42 Library of Congress/Corbis Historical/Getty Images; p. 45 Culture Club/Hulton Archive/Getty Images; p. 59 Moviestore collection Ltd/Alamy Stock Photo; p. 62 Interfoto/Alamy Stock Photo; p. 66 © Lifestyle pictures/Alamy Stock Photo; pp. 68, 72 AF archive/Alamy Stock Photo; p. 75 Haywood Magee/Picture Post/Getty Images; pp. 78, 82, 87 7831/Gamma-Rapho/Getty Images; p. 88 Alex Livesey/FIFA/Getty Images; p. 95 Buyenlarge/Moviepix/Getty Images.

CONTENTS

J. R. R. Tolkien

Literary Roots

"I object to the contemporary trend in criticism, with its excessive interest in the details of the lives of authors and artists. They only distract attention from an author's work."[1]

—J. R. R. Tolkien

John Ronald Reuel Tolkien was born in 1892 in Bloemfontein, one of the capital cities of South Africa. His father was a banking executive who had been transferred from England to South Africa for work. When Tolkien (known as "Ronald" in his early years) was four years old he accompanied his mother and brother back to England to visit family. Tolkien's father was going to follow soon after, but he died of a sudden illness in South Africa, leaving Tolkien's mother to fend for the family. She moved them to a little town near Birmingham, England, called Sarehole, where young Ronald learned to love the British countryside: trees, flowers, fields, forests, and streams. His mother homeschooled him and his brother; she also died young, of diabetes (which was not a treatable disease at the time) when Tolkien was only twelve. The boys were brought up by his mother's friend, a Catholic priest named Francis Morgan, who taught them the texts, beliefs, and morality of the Catholic faith.

Perhaps the most significant event in Tolkien's life, apart from his marriage to Edith Mary Bratt in 1916, was his participation in World War I. He was wary of the war and didn't immediately want to participate, but after finishing college, he did as so many young men did: he enlisted. Tolkien, a lieutenant, led a battalion in France during the Battle of the Somme, one of the bloodiest and darkest skirmishes of an already horrifying war. The war raged across Europe and claimed millions of lives. It was perhaps the largest and most catastrophic war in human history; it remains one of the most traumatic. Men fought in muddy trenches, they ran through barbed wire, and faced newly-invented machine guns, destructive mortar shells, and rifle fire. They died in droves

British troops fight in the trenches at the Battle of the Somme. Tolkien fought in the offensive but became ill and missed much of the 141-day battle, which claimed over 400,000 British lives.

from the ravages of disease. The Battle of the Somme alone lasted several months and claimed almost 1.5 million lives. Tolkien survived the carnage—he fell ill and was evacuated before his battalion was wiped out—but many of his closest college friends did not.

If we look at Tolkien's literature, we will find numerous ways to connect events from his childhood and youth to the themes and events in his stories. The Shire, for example, is the place in Middle-earth where the hobbits live, and it is full of green, goodness, peace, and harmony. The Shire represents everything that grows, that is natural, and that is happy in the world. This affinity for country life is clearly influenced by Tolkien's childhood in Sarehole; even the name "Bag End," Bilbo and Frodo Baggins's home in the Shire, is lifted from Tolkien's aunt's farm of the same name. Sauron and the forces of darkness encourage war and industry, forces that are directly opposed to the idyllic country life of the Shire. If we wanted to psychoanalyze the Tolkien stories, we could begin there: Tolkien is reaching back to the happiness of his childhood, to regain his youth through the epic tales of heroism and virtue in *The Lord of the Rings*.

> **epic**
>
> One of the oldest narrative genres, originally a long poem depicting a heroic quest, now simply refers to long works with heroes.

But this is exactly what Tolkien did not want us to do. He felt that if we tried to understand literature through the life of an author, we'd be distracted from what was really important: the stories themselves. So, while much is known about Tolkien's life story, the question remains: Is it profitable to pay close attention to the links between his biography and his literature? What is gained by this, and what is lost?

What we can gain is an appreciation for the deep historical roots of Tolkien's new mythologies, which are "literary," but also much more than that. Each novel and supporting story of Middle-earth evokes still more, unspoken and unwritten historical and linguistic knowledge. We are constantly being reminded of the ancient epochs of Middle-earth and also of the intricate cultural creations of its creatures. We can cite examples of this almost at random. Upon encountering Fangorn Forest during events in book two of *The Lord of the Rings: The Two Towers*, Legolas and Aragorn comment on their dark, eerie surroundings:

> 'You have journeyed further than I,' said Legolas. 'I have heard nothing of this in my own land, save only songs that tell how the Onodrim, that Men call Ents, dwelt there long ago; for Fangorn is old, old even as the Elves would reckon it.'

> 'Yes, it is old,' said Aragorn, 'as old as the forest by the Barrow-downs, and it is far greater. Elrond says that the two are akin, the last strongholds of the mighty woods of the Elder Days, in which the Firstborn roamed while Men still slept. Yet Fangorn holds some secret of its own. What it is I do not know.'[2]

The catalog of names—onodrim, ents, Fangorn, Barrow-downs, Elrond, the Firstborn—adds to the sense, even if we aren't familiar with the specifics, that there is a tangible historical record, that centuries and millennia accompanied the languages and traditions of these creatures and places. Added to this sense of age and history, the dark forest that the travelers find themselves in is also full of secrets, a mystery that escapes even these wise, experienced warriors. As readers, we can't help but feel a shiver of excitement at the expanse of time and the magic of the unknown that Tolkien helps us imagine.

For all his success and fame with general readers, Tolkien has generally been a critical failure. Literary critics tend to think that Tolkien's stories are overblown, overwritten, confusing, and archaic. Almost any critical history of his works will begin with a litany of terrible reviews or controversies over his fame. For example, regarding *The Lord of the Rings*, "Why was this 'balderdash' so popular, Edmund Wilson asked himself, in *The Nation* (14 April 1956). Well, he concluded, it was because 'certain people—especially, perhaps, in Britain have a life-long appetite for juvenile trash.'"[3] More recently, despite being voted by British readers as the greatest novel of the twentieth century, a *Guardian* reviewer called it "one of the worst books ever written."[4] In a response to an enormously positive literary biography of Tolkien by Tom Shippey, another *Guardian* reviewer notes that

> After the annihilating traumas of the last century,
> it's merely perverse to ascribe greatness to this airy
> but strangely simplified mock-Teutonic never-never
> land, where races and species intermingle at will and
> great battles are fought but there is never any remotely
> convincing treatment of those fundamental human
> concerns through which all societies ultimately define
> themselves—religion, philosophy, politics and the
> conduct of sexual relationships.[5]

In other words, the reviewer believes that *The Lord of the Rings* cannot stand up to the great works of literature that confront the actual complexities of the human experience in love, spiritual thought, ideas, or community. There is love in Tolkien, but it is abstract and ritualized. There is religion, but it is artificial and unconnected to actual faith. And so on. This

One early critic of Tolkien complained that the author "describes a tremendous conflict between good and evil...but his good people are consistently good, his evil figures immovably evil."

reviewer is arguing that what Tolkien accomplished was highly entertaining, but ultimately not great literature.

I don't want to drown Tolkien before we even have a chance to consider his works, but we cannot end a critical review without making reference to Harold Bloom, a Yale professor of literature and one of the most prolific critics in the English language. He seems to have an opinion on just about every book, and he seems to have read just about everything. (If this seems like an exaggeration, just peruse his book *The Western Canon*, in which he lays out a huge list of all the books that belong to the great Western tradition, with a justification for why they belong.) His introduction to a collection of critical essays on Tolkien typifies critical disdain or lack of enthusiasm for Tolkien's work. Bloom notes that he has "aesthetic doubts about Tolkien's trilogy" since it is "inflated, over-written, tendentious, and moralistic in the extreme."[6] Bloom also claims that Tolkien's style is "stiff, false-archaic, over-wrought, and finally a real hindrance in Volume III, *The Return of the King*, which I have had trouble rereading."[7] Upon quoting a paragraph from that book, Bloom seems to give up: "I am not able to understand how a skilled and mature reader can absorb about fifteen hundred pages of this quaint stuff."[8] His adjective "quaint" could easily stand in for harsher, less printable language. In

canon

A set of texts generally agreed to be the most important for a particular culture.

tendentious

Promoting a particular cause or (usually controversial) point of view.

moralistic

Emphasizing moral lessons or teachings.

13

introducing us to scholarship on *The Lord of the Rings*, Bloom breezily dismisses it.

What should we make of all this negativity from literary critics? Given that Tolkien's works are still hugely popular with general readers, one response could be: Who cares what the critics say? Isn't the reading public more important than some self-important professors? Perhaps. But it is probably more important for us to place Tolkien's work in context, and to understand the extent that it influenced modern popular culture. Let us assume that the stories are compelling—many of them are, absolutely—and that they stand up to scrutiny and analysis—most of them do, without a doubt. The fact that they are seen as "for children" probably hurts them in literary circles, but what truly is a "children's" story? Isn't it just a good story? And anyway, isn't it true that children sometimes have *better* equipment for approaching stories than adults? Ursula K. Leguin, commenting on dreams, literature, fantasy, and Tolkien, notes that as a young girl of ten she "certainly wouldn't have gone on about reason and repression and all that. I had no critical equipment, no detachment, and even less power of sustained conscious mind than I have now. But I had as much, or more, of an unconscious mind, and was perhaps in better touch with it than I am now. And it was to that, to the unknown depths in me, that the story spoke."[9] The "childishness" of Tolkien is perhaps an asset.

So let us break with these critics and admit that Tolkien has achieved something noteworthy, that his work has left a deep and lasting mark on popular fiction (and film), and that despite its flaws it deserves the massive popularity it enjoys.

Not all critics are wary of Tolkien, though. He has important and influential defenders, including his friends C. S. Lewis and W. H. Auden, and a long list of literary scholars who have published articles and books analyzing his work in incredible detail. While Harold Bloom may question whether he is an author "for the coming century,"[10] we may find that Tolkien's insistence on environmental ethics, his commitment to what is good and right, and his skepticism of industrial technology, among other fundamental themes, are exactly what is missing in an age of instant communication, high speed travel, long distance warfare, and global risk.

A Life of Fairy-Stories

Tolkien studied English Language and Literature at Exeter College, part of the Oxford University system, earning his undergraduate degree in 1915, just before enlisting in the fight against Germany in World War I. Studying in college, Tolkien began to specialize in a field of research known as philology, or, the genealogical study of words and language. Philologists trace words through cultural and grammatical usage and look for links and overlaps among different languages. This kind of historical research requires unusual focus and attention to detail, but it also requires broad knowledge of mythology, literature, and how people a long time ago used or misused language. Tolkien had been fascinated by the structure and sound of language since he was a young boy; he had invented his first language while still in elementary school and had several smaller languages devised by the time he reached university.

After earning his degree, Tolkien began work on what would eventually become his first elvish language, Quenya. As Gilliver and Marshall note, "[Quenya] had not only an invented vocabulary and grammar but, significantly, an invented linguistic history. The lexicon adopts a thoroughly 'philological' approach, grouping words together under their 'roots', and is therefore no mere wordlist, but aims to be a true (if entirely fictional) etymological dictionary."[1] His interest in natural and invented languages runs through his fiction, in

Tolkien in 1911, the year he began his linguistic studies at Exeter College in Oxford

which you can find the elvish languages Quenya and Sindarin, as well as less developed languages spoken by dwarves, men, orcs, ents, and Sauron, who invents the Black Speech for all the beings in Mordor. (It is interesting that Sauron, the great evil antagonist of *The Lord of the Rings*, is explicitly a language-creator; Tolkien's mirror image appears in both the creative impulses of the elves and the evil of Mordor.)

After the war Tolkien joined a small band of scholars and researchers working on the first edition of the *Oxford English Dictionary (OED)*. The *OED* project had been launched by the Philological Society of London in 1857 to supplement what were then standard dictionaries of English, but were obviously incomplete.[2] Sixty years later, several sections of the project had been published, but a complete edition had not yet been released.[3] Tolkien worked to unravel the etymological histories of words like "walrus," "walnut," and "wan." During his tenure at the *OED*, Tolkien sharpened his philological skills and deepened his knowledge of Old and Middle English. By the time he began teaching literature and mythology at Oxford, Tolkien was well-positioned to produce some of his most enduring academic work.

Tolkien crafted *A Middle English Vocabulary* in 1922, a dictionary of Middle English words, both common and uncommon, along with etymological and philological reference material. This work, long considered authoritative, shows once

etymological

Having to do with the origins of a word.

lexicon

The vocabulary of a language.

philology

The study of the history of language.

more what a detail-oriented and focused scholar of languages Tolkien was. He also translated the fourteenth-century poem *Sir Gawain and the Green Knight,* as well as two other early English poems: *Pearl* and *Sir Orfeo. Sir Gawain* recounts a moral test that Sir Gawain, a knight at King Arthur's Round Table, undergoes: a mysterious green giant challenges any knight to swing his axe at him, a free shot, if the knight agrees to have the blow returned in a year and a day. The test for Gawain is: Will he show up? And will he be honorable, virtuous, and chivalrous until he has met his part of the bargain? He upholds his nobility in the face of death and temptation. This morality tale is an example of ancient source material that influenced Tolkien's later fiction; the courtly love of his often-noble, chivalric characters (for example, Aragorn and Arwen) and the moral tests that many characters must endure (Frodo and Sam under the weight of the Ring) are notable features of *The Lord of the Rings.*

An illustration shows the Knights of the Round Table heading off on a quest. The stories of these brave characters from the Middle Ages inspired Tolkien to create his own tales of epic adventures.

THE INKLINGS, AN EPIC BOOK CLUB

One significant literary influence on Tolkien was his association with a group of scholars and friends, an informal club they affectionately called the Inklings. The group met in Tolkien's or C. S. Lewis's college rooms at Oxford and also regularly at the Eagle and Child pub. The group met in the 1930s and 1940s for informal discussion of literature and language, as well as readings of the works in progress of its members.[4] Tolkien was a founding member; it was with the Inklings that he shared early versions of *The Lord of the Rings*. C. S. Lewis was also a member, and their friendship and mutual support had a significant impact on both authors. It was Tolkien who brought Lewis to his Christian faith (for which he is a famous apologist); that religious thought went on to shape Lewis's *Chronicles of Narnia* tales. Tolkien's son Christopher also joined the group, setting up his status as literary and philosophical heir. Far less well known today, novelist Charles Williams is usually the "third wheel" mentioned alongside Tolkien and Lewis. Through these three authors, though, the club would go on to have an outsize influence on fantasy and science fiction.

One of Tolkien's major accomplishments went unpublished until 2014, decades after his death: a masterful translation of the Old English poem *Beowulf*. And while he never saw fit to publish the translation while he was alive, Tolkien nevertheless drew deep inspiration from this old story of a hero, a dragon, and a monster named Grendel. His essay "Beowulf: the Monsters and the Critics," delivered first as a lecture in 1936, has had a major impact on *Beowulf* scholarship in particular, but it also contains a number of themes that continue throughout Tolkien's wider interests—in fairy tales, for example—as well as the novels and stories he produced.

Beowulf was written in Old English sometime between 700 and 1000 CE (or AD). It is set in Northern Europe, known today as Scandinavia. The protagonist, Beowulf, is a heroic warrior who fights a monster called Grendel after the creature attacks the stronghold of the Danish king Hrothgar.

Tolkien helped his fellow Oxford professor C. S. Lewis (pictured) rediscover his religion. In return, Lewis inspired and supported his friend's long struggle to complete his tales of Middle-earth.

Beowulf also defeats Grendel's mother. Returning to his home, Beowulf is made king of the Geats (his people), and as an old warrior he kills a dragon who has come to terrorize them. The dragon, though, wounds him; Beowulf dies and is memorialized through ritual and verse. Of all the academic work of his career, Tolkien probably drew the most artistic inspiration from *Beowulf*. He uses Norse and Old English languages as guides for his invented tongues, and Beowulf is a powerful model for some of Tolkien's own epic characters, like Aragorn.

Fairy Tales

What should strike any reader of Tolkien's body of fictional work is its remarkable amount of detail. Standing back, taking stock of it, especially *The Hobbit*, *The Lord of the Rings*, and *The Silmarillion*, we get the impression that we are looking at an entire world, comprehensive and coherent in itself, even if it is not exhaustive. In other words, we don't know *everything* about Middle-earth that there is to know, but we know quite a lot. Tolkien has given us a world populated with a vast array of species, spirits, and forces; he's invented several languages that influence the history, names, and stories of that realm; he's constructed a world that is like a looking-glass version of our own. There are similar physics, for example. Objects fall to the ground, things need wings to fly, and arrows are projected from bows, just like in the real world. But on Middle-earth there are magical elements that either do not exist here, or are hidden. Middle-earth is the setting of a complex fairy-story.

Tolkien had a rich understanding of fairy-stories, or fairy tales. On March 8, 1939, Tolkien gave a lecture at the

> **apologist**
>
> One who defends something or someone in writing or speech.

University of St. Andrews in Scotland entitled, very succinctly, "On Fairy-Stories." He later expanded and published his lecture as an essay with the same title. It is Tolkien's attempt to defend the fairy

reductionism

The act of breaking down a complex idea into a very simple form.

tale from a certain kind of reductionism and explain why he thinks fairy tales are important and useful in contemporary society. A careful reading of this essay will provide a crucial key for understanding Tolkien's purpose and techniques in his major works.

What is a fairy tale—or fairy-story, in Tolkien's terms—at its most basic? It'd be pretty obvious to say: A fairy-story is a

The Fairies' Song in Midsummer Night's Dream, from an 1890 Shakespeare collection. Fairies and other magical creatures were a favorite topic of storytellers long before Tolkien featured them in his works.

story about fairies. But Tolkien isn't satisfied with this answer, and points out that it introduces a number of extra questions. For example, what is a fairy? How do we account for all the other elements of fairy stories? And what is the function of the storytelling part of a fairy story? Fairies, Tolkien notes, are generally thought of as tiny little creatures, but this is wrong. Fairies are elves, and elves are versions of humans. Magical people, over time, shrunk down in size as Europeans learned more and more about the globe and about other cultures. Tolkien explains:

> I suspect that this flower-and-butterfly minuteness was ... a product of '"rationalisation", which transformed the glamour of Elf-land into mere finesse, and invisibility into a fragility that could hide in a cowslip or shrink behind a blade of grass. It seems to become fashionable soon after the great voyages had begun to make the world seem too narrow to hold both men and elves; when the magic land of *Hy Breasail* in the West had become the mere Brazils, the land of red-dye-wood.[5]

In other words, elves and fairies lost their standing in direct proportion to the triumph of science and exploration. The more the world appeared to the European cultures as reasonable, knowable, full of facts and systems, the fewer mysteries it contained and the power of magic seemed to diminish. What used to be a mythical forest over the Western ocean became a colony that produced the raw materials for commerce.

Tolkien is clearly critical of this trend, so much so that in his own fictional fairy world, Middle-earth, the elves are grand, tall, and powerful. But there are many qualities of traditional fairy-stories that he retains in his own writing, qualities of which he's very conscious. For instance, a fairy-story is not just about fairies. It is about "Faërie," "the realm or state in which fairies have their being."[6] It is a kind of parallel or "extra"-natural realm that contains fairies and "dwarves, witches, trolls ... dragons" but also the things of nature that hold deep significance for humans: "the seas, the sun, the moon, the sky; and the earth, and all things that are in it: tree and bird, water and stone, wine and bread, and ourselves, mortal men, when we are enchanted."[7] These stories are deeply embedded in nature and the natural world; that is where all the magic of fairy-stories and Tolkien's own fantasy work originates.

The struggle at stake in the fairy world is between good and evil, perhaps, but more importantly it is about the conflict between nature and machine, mystery and science, dreams and reality. In Tolkien's opinion, "*Faërie* itself may perhaps most nearly be translated by Magic—but it is magic of a peculiar mood and power, at the furthest pole from the vulgar devices of the laborious, scientific, magician."[8] We will see this played out in Tolkien's major works, *The Hobbit* and *The Lord of the Rings*. The power of evil in Middle-earth is always generated through industrial processes or methods that go against what we might call "natural": mass deforestation, digging deep mines and production facilities, or corrupting the processes of generation and birth to breed hideously powerful beasts.

We can read Tolkien's attitude to nature and natural forces throughout his body of work, and it projects a desire to maintain a form of Romanticism by embracing the natural and rejecting that which he sees as unnatural. But what else does this accomplish? In effect, Tolkien is setting up a dichotomy that might be artificial. Why, for instance, is a spider's web considered natural, while the Internet—another "web" of sorts—would be considered unnatural? In fact, why can't something like the Internet even be thought of as *magical*? This is because in Western culture, including the British culture by which Tolkien was shaped, there is a clear distinction between human and nature. Man is set above all other animals and non-human objects. The underlying belief is that there is a very special quality to humans that other animals don't have, a part of us that is a soul or a higher form of consciousness. Whether or not this is true, what we can establish is that the human/nature split is culturally constructed, not objective fact of any kind. The split is a way of thinking that is encouraged and reinforced by literature, film, and other images and ways of speaking. Tolkien's works tend to sentimentalize "nature" and hint at the sorrow that humans must face after having fallen away from their original natural state, in paradise. (We will refer back to this sentimentalizing tendency when we discuss *The Silmarillion* in Chapter 2, and Tolkien's understanding of "the fall" in storytelling.) They are a part of the cultural apparatus that maintains the division between humans and nature.

---

dichotomy

A contrast between two things that are assumed to be separate or opposite

---

Trees vs. Machines: Romanticism and the Enlightenment

In the late eighteenth century, at about the time of the American Declaration of Independence from Great Britain and the explosion of the French Revolution, an intellectual movement had been brewing that we know as the Enlightenment. That term refers to a loosely associated collection of thinkers, texts, philosophies, and governments. In effect, the Enlightenment represented the triumph of science and reason in the world. Gone were the dark days of ritual, myth, and mysterious beliefs that held sway during the Middle Ages in Europe.

What Enlightenment thinkers wanted was an age of reason, one where government was democratic and systematic, and where all other areas of social life were rationalized. For example, business and economics would be better defined, regulated, and encouraged through rational approaches to trade and tariffs. Medicine changed from an art to a science where the body could be seen as a machine, and thus repaired and maintained like a machine. The Industrial Revolution was booming, increasing the speed of transportation and bringing people together under a unified worldview. Education was standardized more and more. Everything could, in principle, using the tools of science, be known. The universe would open its secrets to human inquiry. The dream of the Enlightenment was to make the world a more rational place, and thus a more peaceful place.

Opposed to this trend was a way of thinking and creating that came to be known as Romanticism. Romanticism emphasized the natural, the sublime (overwhelming natural power and beauty; like a giant mountain, a powerful river, or a massive waterfall), and the mysterious. Not everything could be known, Romantics claimed. Art, and the sublime feelings it caused, would always exceed the rationalization of the world. This didn't mean that science was worthless, but only that it couldn't achieve its ultimate goal of knowing and explaining *everything*. Romantics tended to be poets or religious figures, but they were also scientists and politicians. Again, "Romanticism" was not a term used in the 1790s, but was applied retrospectively to account for these two major intellectual trends.

The tension between Enlightenment ideals and Romanticism plays out in many contemporary situations, but for Tolkien it is most clearly represented by his use of the nature–

Jean-Jacques Rousseau is considered the founding father of Romanticism, a philosophy that Tolkien seems to embrace when he equates industry with evil forces.

machine conflict. What is mechanical or machine-driven is what is highly rational, reasoned, and scientific. The machine is indifferent to its own functions; the machine doesn't care what the input is, nor what the output is, only that it runs and *produces*. The dark forces of Sauron and Saruman rely heavily on industrial machinery to produce their military strength. This is highlighted in the second book of the *Lord of the Rings* trilogy, *The Two Towers*, in which Saruman enrages the ents (ancient tree-beings) by cutting down Fangorn Forest to feed his industrial ambitions. Treebeard, one of the old ents, noting how much Saruman has changed, realizes: "I think that I now understand what he is up to. He is plotting to become a Power. He has a mind of metal and wheels; and he does not care for growing things, except as far as they serve him for the moment."[9] The trees he destroys are going to feed the "fires of Orthanc," Saruman's explosive bomb-like weapon. These comments illustrate how Tolkien sets up an explicit conflict— an actual *war*, the Battle of Isengard—between the ancient life of trees and the fiery machines that consume and burn. We can detect a temporal (having to do with time) conflict here, too, in the sense that ents (and trees in general) move very slowly, where machines and fire are characterized by velocity.

The ents are among several creatures in Middle-earth that emphasize a kind of deep ecology, but they are also part of a continuum of environmentalism. In *Ents, Elves, and Eriador*, Dickerson and Evans argue that there are a range of "environmental stewards" who represent different aspects of what it means to care about and take care of the environment. Tom Bombadil, the hobbits, Gandalf, and the elves, among others, represent "the benevolent, selfless custodial care of the environment"[10] that reflects a need for community—we must act together—and personal responsibility—"we do what we can" (says Treebeard the Ent).[11] Aside from transforming natural resources into personal gain, Dickerson and Evans point out, Sauron and Saruman both forgo any kind of council or communal decision making; they violate both the central qualities of stewardship of their opponents. In the end, even though there is much of what resembles "natural magic" in these stories, the Tolkien model of environmentalism is very pragmatic.

Interestingly, the clash between Romanticism and Enlightenment ideals in Tolkien has been criticized for being weighted too heavily in favor of Romantic nature worship. After all, the objection goes, aren't science and reason still powerful forces for shaping peace and prosperity? Hasn't medical science developed new and important treatments and surgeries? Hasn't engineering science come up with new ways of communicating, traveling, and learning? A novel published in 1999 by Russian author Kirill Yeskov, *The Last Ringbearer*, tells an alternative history of Middle-earth in which Sauron and the industry of Mordor are not "evil", but are working to modernize production and achieve progressive reforms through technology and industry. Gandalf is depicted as a fanatical imperialist, a conservative oppressor who wants to hold back the imaginative and productive progress of scientific rationalism. A conversation in that novel between Saruman and Gandalf serves to undermine the simplistic links between nature and goodness, technology and evil:

> [GANDALF:] "The Middle-earth is a multitude of peoples living in harmony with nature and the heritage of their ancestors now ...

> [SARUMAN:] "... Every generation of wizards is weaker than the previous one, so sooner or later Men will face

Nature alone. And then they will need Science and Technology—provided you haven't eradicated those by then."

[Gandalf:] "They don't need your science, for it destroys the harmony of the World and dries up the souls of men!"

[Saruman:] "Strange is the talk of Soul and Harmony on the lips of a man who is about to start a war. As for science, it is dangerous not to them, but to you—or, rather, to your warped self-esteem. What are we wizards but consumers of that which our predecessors had created, while they are creators of new knowledge? We face the Past, they face the Future."[12]

What Yeskov has captured in this exchange is the subtlety of nature-technology conflicts. From a certain perspective, fighting to maintain a "state of nature" is a violent project since it rejects what are essentially progressive innovations and technologies. For example, should medicine be rewound back to the way it was practiced in pre-industrial days? Should communications technology be un-invented, destroyed, outlawed? Should we stop any cultural progress that doesn't support the reclaiming of "nature"? The Saruman of *The Last Ringbearer* sees what Tolkien seems to miss in *The Lord of the Rings*: that if we really are opposing nature and technology, it would be a totalitarian move to destroy technology. Given that *Ringbearer* was written in Russia makes this insight even more ironic, since Russia's political history is bound tightly to the history of modern totalitarianism in the form of Communism and the current militant regime of Vladimir Putin.

Tolkien makes this part of his project explicit in a letter to his editor (regarding *The Silmarillion*, see chapter 2 for more). The elves, according to Tolkien, are artists, so-called "sub-creators," and "their 'magic' is Art, delivered from many of its human limitations: more effortless, more quick, more complete ... And its object is Art not Power, sub-creation not domination and tyrranous re-forming of Creation."[13] What industry brings is not, for Tolkien, a better world, but one in which the forces of progress work to dominate nature and other beings. "The Enemy in successive forms is always 'naturally' concerned with sheer Domination, and so the Lord of magic and machines; but the problem: that this frightful evil can and does arise from an apparently good root, the desire to benefit the world and others—speedily and according to the benefactor's own plans—is a recurrent motive."[14] This is a sophisticated problem: what we think of as progress—which involves invention, innovation, and that which is "new"—is the mask that hides the power and domination at work in industrial society. Art, though, can always and only be "for itself" and "for its own sake." The problem, though, with "art for art's sake" is that art is never simply complete in itself; it has political and moral implications, just as Tolkien's own novels and stories do (despite his arguments that they are disconnected from their context and any authorial intention). This is the philosophical complexity at work in the "good versus evil" simplicity of Middle-earth.

THE SILMARILLION

*T*he *Silmarillion* is a strange, complex, and difficult text. Tolkien did not write it from start to finish, but rather in fits and starts over the course of almost fifty years. The stories and legends contained in it were drafted and abandoned and rewritten and tweaked, but never published while Tolkien was alive. In some ways, no one would have taken it seriously until they'd been drawn in by *The Hobbit* and *The Lord of the Rings*. As a reader of these more traditional novelistic narratives, it is a thrilling experience to learn the deep, mysterious background to the events, characters, and prophecies of the Rings of Power, wizards, elves, dwarves, orcs, and the great evil that threatens all of Middle-earth. *The Silmarillion* allows us to see that the events of *The Lord of the Rings* are a significant but relatively small aspect of a larger, grander universe of forces.

Tolkien never published *The Silmarillion* mainly because his editors were not convinced that it was publishable, whatever "it" was. After his death in 1973, his son Christopher undertook the editing and curation of the vast amount of unpublished material his father left behind, including these early historical-mythological narratives. According to Christopher, "throughout my father's long life he never abandoned it, nor ceased even in his last years to work on it."[1] But Tolkien never considered the text a single, unchanging object that he could "finish." He worked on different stories, sometimes writing them as poems, then rewriting them as prose, lengthening or shortening them as his views developed.

> As the years passed the changes and variants, both in detail and in larger perspectives, became so complex, so pervasive, and so many-layered that a final and definitive version seemed unattainable ... In his later writing mythology and poetry sank down behind his theological and philosophical preoccupations: from which arose incompatibilities of tone.[2]

It was up to Tolkien's son to put it all together, to publish something that would make some kind of sense to a reader, that wouldn't obscure the important central feelings and ideas in the stories. The result was the text Christopher published in 1977, four years after the death of its author.

Some portions of the text—*Of Túrin Turambar*, for example—had to be completed before they were published since Tolkien left threads loose and untied. In this work and in cleaning up and organizing the piles of notebooks and drafts, Christopher enlisted the help of a young student—a friend of the Tolkien family from Canada—named Guy Gavriel Kay. Kay would emerge from that year of intensive editing a stronger writer, and the experience inspired his own renowned career as a fantasy and historical fiction writer. And while he still won't disclose many details about the process—the entire compilation of *The Silmarillion* was done in utmost secrecy—in an interview with the *Guardian* Kay reflects that working with Christopher Tolkien allowed him to see that what we read, the amazing stories and complex historical systems, only came about through a long series of failures and "false-starts."

> You learn that the great works have disastrous botched chapters, that the great writers recognise that they didn't

In the 1970s, Guy Gavriel Kay (pictured) assisted Christopher Tolkien in the completion of *The Silmarillion*. The Canadian writer is now known for his own fantasy works, which are often based on actual historical times and places.

work. So I was looking at drafts of *The Lord of the Rings* and rough starts for *The Silmarillion* and came to realise they don't spring full-blown, utterly, completely formed in brilliance. They get there with writing and rewriting and drudgery and mistakes, and eventually if you put in the hours and the patience, something good might happen.[3]

Importantly, beyond being inspired to make mistakes in the pursuit of greatness, we can also learn from the publication history of *The Silmarillion* that literature is an organic, living thing. That is, a text is meaningful in different ways and in different times, and as more material related to these particular tales are published, the stories change and grow. Randel Helms puts it nicely when he asks, "What, really, *is* a literary work? Is it what the author intended (or may have intended) it to be, or is it what a later editor makes of it?"[4] We can add, or is it what the reader makes of it, or what many different readers make of it in different time periods and different cultural situations? (This experience is easy to test: simply read a children's book that you used to love as a child, like *Winnie the Pooh* or *Curious George*, and now that you are older and wiser, consider your reaction to it and what it means to you. Think about how much you and the text are *different* than you were before.) Crucially, as Christopher Tolkien acknowledges, "there is no 'real' *Silmarillion*; it died as a dream and a plan in the mind of Tolkien."[5]

The function of the text is to provide historical and mythological background to the events of *The Lord of the Rings*, and generally to establish some of the larger themes of that text. Even though Tolkien conceived of these tales and myths long before he wrote *The Lord of the Rings*, Christopher Tolkien's edition of *The Silmarillion*, which is heavily edited and "constructed" from numerous versions and variations, wasn't published until after the novels. Thus, despite the chronology of authorship and Tolkien's own understanding of his body of work, and because of the way that most readers approach Tolkien's works (they read the novels first), *The Silmarillion* is often read as a "supporting" text rather than a central project.

Plot

The text is divided into five main parts: "Ainulindalë," "Valaquenta," "Quenta Silmarillion," "Akallabêth," and "Of the Rings of Power and the Third Age." Of these, the "Quenta Silmarillion" is the longest and most complex, although each has its own purpose and role to play in the larger legendary scope of Middle-earth.

"Ainulindalë," translated from the Quenya language as "Music of the Ainur", is a cosmogony, or a creation account. It closely resembles well-known creation stories from other cultures and religions, especially the book of Genesis from the Old Testament of the Bible. In the beginning, it explains, "there was Eru, the One, who in Arda [Middle-earth] is called Ilúvatar." Ilúvatar is like God of the Old Testament in that he reigns over a host of angelic figures known as Ainur. Tolkien's twist on Judeo-Christian cosmogony is that instead of going about the tasks of creation right away, Ilúvatar and the Ainur begin making music: Ilúvatar establishes the theme, and the Ainur use their creativity and imagination to create variations and harmonies on the theme. This "Great Music" acts as the creative force to bring the universe into being:

> A sound arose of endless interchanging melodies woven
> in harmony that passed beyond hearing into the depths
> and into the heights, and the places of the dwelling of
> Ilúvatar were filled to overflowing, and the music and the

echo of the music went out into the Void, and it was not void.[6]

Out of this harmony arises the first instances of discord, dissonance, and what will be seen as evil: Melkor, the most talented and powerful of all the Ainur, decides that he wants his part to be more important than other parts, so he begins introducing melodies that run counter to the overall theme established by Ilúvatar.

Melkor's rebellion is significant because in a sense it represents in miniature the entire future of Middle-earth. Like Lucifer in the Old Testament, Melkor wants independence and the power of personal creation. As Melkor contemplates the emptiness of the universe, "desire grew hot within him to bring into Being things of his own, and it seemed to him that Ilúvatar took no thought for the Void, and he was impatient of its emptiness ... [B]eing alone he had begun to conceive thoughts of his own unlike those of his brethren."[7] At the heart of all evil, then, is desire, but if we read carefully we can't ignore the fact that Melkor's desire is a desire to create, which was his original task. His desire is to be original, to shape his own future, to make the universe grow. In a word, his desire is *good*. But since it is a desire for *radical* individuality, the kind of individuality that refuses to acknowledge something greater than itself, it leads him down a dark path to shame, anger, and hatred.

cosmogony thesis

A cosmic creation story or theory.

After reestablishing themes to counter Melkor's discordant variations, Ilúvatar stops the music and reveals what it is they have been creating: Middle-earth, which they call Arda, including the "Children of Ilúvatar," elves and men.

In revealing this to the Ainur, Ilúvatar makes the point that even Melkor's attempts to separate himself from the universal whole were in vain: everyone's thoughts and variations are part of the greater plan. Many of the Ainur decide to go to Arda and help with its development; they become the Valar, the Powers of the World, a sort of pantheon of gods. Each Vala has certain strengths and specialties, much like the specialization of ancient Greek and Roman gods. They might connect to various emotions such as patience or joy, or active qualities like craftsmanship or gardening, or elements like the sea, the earth, or the wind. The book ends with the first war between the Valar and Melkor for control of the new world, in preparation for the coming of elves and men.

"Valaquenta" is less a creation myth than it is a catalog of important characters and their characteristics. We learn detailed accounts of the various Valar and their relationships with each other. A cast of characters emerges: Manwë becomes the King of the Valar; Ulmo controls the seas and waterways; Melkor distances himself from the Valar and becomes his own opposing dark force; and so on. We also learn about the Maiar, a class of beings slightly less powerful than the Valar, like the lieutenants. Among these is Olórin, described as "wisest of the Maiar," who learns pity and patience from a Vala named Nienna, and who eventually becomes "the friend of all the Children of Ilúvatar." When Olórin speaks, "those who listened to him awoke from despair and put away the imaginations of darkness."[8] Olórin, we will learn from other sources, is none other than Gandalf the Grey, also known as Mithrandir, one of the principle characters in *The Lord of the Rings*. His status as a Maia manifestation (basically, an angel in human form)—as well as the status of the other wizards Sauron, Saruman and Radagast, and the Balrogs—enhances how that epic is shaped at several levels of power, from the humble hobbit to the mighty sorcerer, and everything in between.

"Quenta Silmarillion"

The first two books act as establishing material, outlining the overlying battle between good and evil, harmony and dissonance, while the third book, "Quenta Silmarillion," is the main body of the text. It adds further depth and complexity to the mythical-historical account of Middle-earth. For instance, Valinor, the holy land where the Valar reside along with the Maiar and the oldest and most powerful elf races, gets a more detailed description. One of the Valar associated with growth and life, Yavanna, creates the Two Trees of Valinor that contain the powerful light of Ilúvatar. These trees seem to establish a kind of gender duality to the world:

> The one had leaves of dark green that beneath were as shining silver, and from each of his countless flowers a dew of silver light was ever falling ... The other bore leaves of a young green like the new-opened beech; their edges were glittering gold. Flowers swung upon her branches in clusters of yellow flame, formed each to a glowing horn that spilled a golden rain upon the ground.[9]

The silver and gold is linked to a male-female dichotomy, and this duality extends to the cycles of day and night: night is governed by the silver light of the moon, day the golden light of the sun. The waning and waxing of the trees' light comes at twelve hour intervals. Thus, day and night are created, and "thus began also the Count of Time."[10]

Aside from time and the power of light, associated with elemental trees (which serve to remind us of the trees in the Garden of Eden, and the Tree of Life in many religious and mythological traditions—see sidebar), we get more detail on elves and men, the Children of Ilúvatar. Elves are "more like in nature to the Ainur, though less in might and stature" so they have the most intimate and direct relationship with the Valar and the Maiar. They are immortal, like their more powerful kin, and are devoted to the creative arts. Men, on the other hand, Ilúvatar "gave strange gifts." When deciding how to populate Arda, Ilúvatar sat back in thought, and then declared that although the elves (also known as the Quendi) would "be the fairest of all earthly creatures" and would "bring forth more beauty than all my Children; and they shall have the greater bliss in this world," men (or Atani) would be given a "new gift." What is this new, and presumably special, gift?

> Therefore, [Ilúvatar] willed that the hearts of Men should
> seek beyond the world and should find no rest therein;
> but they should have a virtue to shape their life, amid the
> powers and chances of the world, beyond the Music of
> the Ainur, which is as fate to all things else.[11]

In other words, men would have a kind of free will that no other creature has. It wouldn't make them happier, necessarily: just freer. This free will would turn into willfulness and stubbornness, and it would make them vulnerable to manipulation by the temptations of Melkor and Sauron. But along with this "gift of freedom," Ilúvatar gave them the "gift" of death: "It is one with this gift of freedom that the children of Men dwell only a short space in the world alive, and are not bound to it, and depart soon whither the Elves knew not."[12] Elves will live until the end of the world, becoming more sorrowful over time, but men would "leave the world."

The "gift" of death was originally one that "even the Powers would envy," but Melkor made death into a terrible, evil

An artist's rendition of the Tree of Life in the Garden of Eden, the site of one of the most classic battles between good and evil.

THE TREE OF LIFE AROUND THE WORLD

The Tree of Life, or the World Tree, is one of the most common mythological symbols in cultures around the world. It is found in ancient Norse traditions—a major source of inspiration for Tolkien's writings, as we've seen so far—in the form of *Yggdrasil*, a giant tree whose branches reach into heaven and roots extend throughout the world. Sacred trees appear in ancient Egyptian mythology as the basis for divine rebirth, and in Native American traditions as a massive tree to connect the four directions and the heavens and the earth. The Lebanese flag features a Lebanon cedar tree in its center, an icon representing the cedar trees prevalent in that region of the Middle East that have come to be associated with rebirth, immortality, and holiness. In the ancient poem, *Epic of Gilgamesh*, one of the first quests that Gilgamesh and Enkidu embark upon is to the forests of Lebanon to steal the valuable cedar trees. Christian myths connect this ancient tradition to more "modern" teachings, including the idea that the Christian cross is (ironically, it seems) analogous to the tree of life.

It is, in fact, difficult to find a human civilization or belief system that did not at some point feature a sacred tree. The worship of trees is still around today in the form of the Christmas tree, an import from pagan (non-Christian) practices of revering the evergreen that does not die in winter. And of course, at the heart of the Garden of Eden are two trees: the Tree of the Knowledge of Good and Evil, and the Tree of Life. The "fall" of humanity is precipitated by humans breaking the rules concerning sacred trees.

Tolkien's variations on this near-universal theme include the Two Trees of Valinor, as well as the white tree of Gondor, which withers as the kingdom falls into decline. When Aragorn returns to claim the throne, symbolically paralleling the messianic return of Jesus Christ in the Biblical tradition, he plants a new Tree of Gondor.

thing, perverting the beauty of the gift, "confounded it with darkness, and brought forth evil out of good, and fear out of hope."[13] In a later chapter titled "On Men," we learn that men are given names like "sickly," "mortals," "usurpers," "strangers," "inscrutable," "self-cursed," "heavy-handed," and "Children of the Sun" (referring to their fear of the dark).[14] Human life, as it is limited, also contains a mystery: "what may befall their spirits after death the Elves knew not."[15] In a provocative statement, the narrator adds that "the fate of Men after death, maybe, is not in the hands of the Valar, nor was all foretold in the Music of the Ainur."[16] This basic mystery at the heart of the cosmos is manifested in human beings, who play a crucial role in producing the key characters (children of elf-human love) who will end up fighting against the darkness.

Themes and Motifs

Dwarves: Biblical Themes of Abraham, Isaac, and Ishmael

In the Book of Genesis, some family troubles end up establishing one of the most important cultural conflicts of our own modern age, among Christian, Jewish, and Islamic faiths and cultures. Abraham has two sons: Ishmael is his first son, born from his slave Hagar (not his wife); Isaac is his first "legitimate" son, born from Sarah, his wife. Abraham favors Isaac, who becomes his direct heir. Ishmael and his mother are pushed out of the way by a jealous Sarah; Ishmael becomes the ancestor of Mohammed and the legendary origin of the Arab peoples. Isaac is the ancestor of Moses and Jesus, thus the legendary origin of the Judeo-Christian peoples. This conflict between Isaac and Ishmael is the symbolic heart of much global conflict today.

In the Bible, Ruth demands that Abraham send away Hagar and Ishmael. In *The Silmarillion*, the dwarves take on the role of Ishmael, the illegitimate children hidden away underground.

Something similar happens with Tolkien's account of the dwarves. Dwarves were not part of the original plan for Arda; Ilúvatar had conceived of the elves and men, but had stopped there. One of the Valar, Aulë, a Power that helped shape Arda in the early days before the Children of Ilúvatar were created, wanted his own race of beings to teach and love. So Aulë secretly creates the dwarves, hiding his work in the caves under the mountains. Ilúvatar is disturbed by Aulë's creation, since the dwarves technically preempt the appearance of the elves, so he orders Aulë to keep the dwarves under the mountain until the elves and men arrive. This rash action on Aulë's part parallels Melkor's desire to create his own melodies. Aulë "took up a great hammer to smite the Dwarves" on Ilúvatar's insistence that he correct his mistake.[17] (This is similar to God ordering Abraham to sacrifice Isaac, his beloved son.) "But Ilúvatar had compassion upon Aulë and his desire" and spares the dwarves in the end. He does warn, however, that "when the time comes I will awaken them, and they shall be to thee as children; and often strife shall arise between thine and mine, the children of my adoption and the children of my choice."[18] The Isaac-Ishmael divide is established between elves and dwarves; this conflict is important in later stories, when the two races are at odds, elves being drawn to beauty, grace, and cultivating green life; dwarves being naturally drawn to stone, mining, metal, and industrial construction.

Animosity between the two races flares when dwarves are hired by the elvish king Thingol to combine the Silmarils, the greatest of the elvish creations, with the Nauglamír, a necklace said to be only the second greatest creation in Arda (second to the Silmarils themselves). After setting one of the recovered jewels in the necklace, the dwarves refuse to return the necklace to Thingol; they murder him instead, precipitating an all-out war between dwarves and elves, and setting the tone for ages of mistrust.

The Silmarils: Desire Turned Evil

The "history of the Silmarils" was conceived by Tolkien as a counterpoint to the story of the rings of power that culminates in *The Lord of the Rings* trilogy. The Silmarils are jewels that contain the Light of Ilúvatar, which is the source of power in the universe, wielded by the Valar, and to a much lesser extent, the Maiar and elves. As a parallel to the story of Melkor's desire for creation leading ultimately to evil, the Silmarils are first created by one of the elves living in Valinor (the land in the West where the Valar and their attendants reside), a powerful and talented figure named Fëanor. As in the case of Melkor's rebellion, Fëanor creates the three Silmarils from a desire to create something more beautiful than anything else in the world. He imbues the gems with light from the Two Trees of Valinor, magical trees that sustain the power of Ilúvatar on Earth. Everyone, including the Valar, considers these gems holy and important objects. And they are considered wonderful and good, until two forces conspire to make them a source of conflict: Fëanor becomes convinced that everyone else, including the Valar themselves, is after his precious jewels; and Melkor attacks Valinor and destroys the Two Trees. This means that the Silmarils are the only remaining vessels of the Light of Ilúvatar on Earth, increasing their value immeasurably. The future of Arda rests on these gems.

What follows from these facts is lengthy and complex; we do not have the time and space to recount even a basic summary of all the relevant information. (You might say that part of the power of Tolkien is that his work resists easy summary. In a way, it's endless.) But by way of making sense of the structure of the text, we should recognize that the Silmarils are the most visible example of great evil resulting from a desire to do great good, thus repeating the theme that Melkor (also known as Morgoth) introduces into the world during the Music of the Ainur. Beyond that overarching theme, however, Tolkien creates some of his most subtle and literary myths

Tolkien's wife of fifty-five years, Edith, was likely his model for Lúthien, who sacrifices her own immortality to be with Beren, the love of her life.

RONALD AND EDITH

Tolkien's love for his wife, Edith, seems to have been deep and lifelong. The two met as teenagers, both orphans living in boarding houses. Edith had an Anglican background, Tolkien was a Catholic. (The friction between the Roman Catholic Church and the Church of England has a long and violent history.) Tolkien's guardian, Father Francis Xavier Morgan, was a Catholic priest, so he told Tolkien he couldn't see Edith until he was twenty-one and an independent adult. Tolkien obeyed, and for years cut off contact with Edith. In the meantime, she had moved away and gotten engaged. When he turned twenty-one, Tolkien promptly wrote Edith a letter asking her to marry him, telling her he still loved her. She immediately dumped her fiancé and agreed to marry Tolkien.[19]

In a letter to his son Christopher after Edith's death, Tolkien admitted that "she was (and knew she was) my Lúthien" and that all the challenges and difficulties they faced together "never touched our depths nor dimmed the memories of our youthful love. For ever (especially when alone) we still met in the woodland glade and went hand in hand many times to escape the shadow of imminent death, before our last parting."[20] Tolkien's reference to the story of Beren and Lúthien underscores the depth of his feeling for this fellow orphan who seemed to complete him and inspire him until the very end.

out of the struggle over the gems. For example, the tragic yet redemptive tale of Beren and Lúthien tells of the love between a mortal man and an immortal female elf. (There is evidence that Tolkien had a special feeling for this particular love story; he is said to have been inspired by his own love for his wife,

Edith. She is referred to as "Lúthien" and he as "Beren" on their shared headstone. See sidebar for more.) Their love is so strong that they are able to carry out a seemingly impossible task (set for them by Lúthien's disapproving father, who doesn't want his daughter to marry a mortal man): to recover one of the Silmarils from the clutches of Morgoth, who has stolen them. Beren is mortally wounded during the mission, and Lúthien pleads with the Valar to bring him back to life. He is brought back, but at the cost of Lúthien's own immortality. They are able to grow old and die together. This tale then forms the basis for later elf-man pairings, including Aragorn and Arwen in *The Lord of the Rings*.

Another of the great and classically-inspired tales of *The Silmarillion* is the story of Túrin Turambar. This tale is a combination of elements: dragon-slaying, curses, tragic love affairs, and a self-sacrificing hero. It was a conscious attempt by Tolkien to rewrite the Norse myth of Kullervo, a similarly cursed warrior from a Finnish epic called the *Kalevala*. Túrin is a son of Húrin, one of the mighty men of the First Age who is captured by Morgoth, kept prisoner, and cursed by the evil lord. Túrin tries to fight Morgoth and to avoid the curse, but in vain. He ends up killing a loyal friend, alienating his allies, and accidentally falling in love with his sister Nienor (who doesn't know that she is his sister, and Túrin doesn't know what she looks like, not having seen her since she was a baby.) The dragon Glaurung perpetrates the deception through a kind of hypnosis. Túrin ultimately kills the dragon, but not before Glaurung reveals to Nienor that she has married her brother. Nienor throws herself off the edge of a cliff, and Túrin likewise kills himself in shame and horror. The mighty warrior brought low by a curse and by fate not only parallels Kullervo, but also the ancient Greek story of Oedipus the King, whose unavoidable fate is to murder his father and marry his mother. These tales are exciting and complex in their battles and intrigues, but also help us work through the themes of free will, destiny, and death that are central to the stories of men on Middle-earth, as well as to our own lives.

Is This Christian Literature?

As part of Tolkien's attempt to convince his publishers that *The Silmarillion* and *The Lord of the Rings* should be published together, or connected, as a long saga of jewels and rings, he wrote a lengthy letter to Milton Waldman at Collins Publishing describing the major themes and threads that run through all these Middle-earth fantasies. It is a valuable document for Tolkien scholars since it very clearly lays out the entire structure of Tolkien's vision. Tolkien's son Christopher, who has been the executor of his literary legacy, obtained a copy of the letter and published it as the preface to *The Silmarillion*. In this letter, Tolkien helps us understand a few specific themes and general theories of storytelling, that he will emphasize in other works on fairy tales, mythology and linguistics.

First, Tolkien's motivation: He has been inventing languages and longing for meaningful legends since he was a small boy. "I do no remember a time when I was not building it," he writes, referring to this huge collection of tales we know as the Middle-earth stories. "Many children make up, or begin to make up, imaginary languages. I have been at it since I could write. But I have never stopped, and of course, as a professional philologist ... I have changed in taste, improved in theory, and probably in craft."[21] But the project was not contained to imagining languages that give "a cohesion, a consistency of linguistic style, and an illusion of historicity" to the stories.[22] Tolkien was trying to create what he felt was missing in the world: "heroic legend on the brink of fairy-tale and history."[23] While he admits that England does have the Arthur legends, which clearly influence Tolkien's own work (compare Merlin the good wizard and Gandalf the good wizard, for example), he notes that there are basic problems with those stories. "For one thing," he writes, "its 'faerie' is too lavish, and fantastical, incoherent and repetitive. For another and more important thing: it is involved in, and explicitly contains the Christian religion."[24]

Why would it matter that the Arthur legends involve Christianity explicitly? While based on ancient Celtic traditions, the Arthur stories were injected with a heavy dose of Christianity during the thirteenth century, in particular after Robert de Boron wrote a newly religious version of the stories, a new version that had a lasting impact. The importation of Christianity spoils them, according to Tolkien. "Myth and fairy-story must, as all art, reflect and contain in solution elements of moral and religious truth (or error), but not explicit, not in the known form of the primary 'real' world."[25] In other words, while myths should animate the same symbols and concepts as religious experience, it shouldn't necessarily be tied directly to those experiences; this limits them to a single context, instead of expanding to a more universal human experience. One of the strengths of Tolkien's work is that it is accessible to so many different cultures and worldviews.

A Christian Framework: The Weak Are Strong

Tolkien's strong Catholic faith imbues his fairy tale with Christian spirit, without the *specific* Christian teachings. The great heroes of Tolkien are the littlest, the weakest, and the least likely. The most obvious example is Frodo Baggins, the hero of *The Lord of the Rings*, but it is reflected in the earliest stories as well. Christian texts are adamant about the links between humility and holiness. In the Gospel of Matthew, for example, Jesus declares that "blessed are the meek; for they shall inherit the earth." (Matt. 5:5) In other words, the powerless will become powerful. (This concept was, incidentally, part of the reason for Jesus's "revolutionary" quality, and since his teachings contradicted the power of Roman authority, they perhaps played a role in his political execution.) German philosopher Georg Hegel makes a similar point in the eighteenth century: that history is ultimately the story of slaves becoming free. Jesus stresses humility and peace in other ways as well. Later in Matthew, Jesus is relating a parable whose moral is that "the last will be first, and the first will be last." (Matt. 20:16) These themes appear in Tolkien, for instance, in the "Story of Beren and Lúthien the Elfmaiden":

> [W]e meet, among other things, the first example of
> the motive (to become dominant in Hobbits) that the
> great policies of world history, "the wheels of the world",
> are often turned not by the Lords and Governors, even
> gods, but by the seemingly unknown and weak—owing
> to the secret life in creation, and the part unknowable to
> all wisdom but One, that resides in the intrusions of the
> Children of God into the Drama.[26]

The love between a man and an elf is strong enough to influence the course of Earth's history in Beren and Lúthien's retrieval of a Silmaril.

Free Will and Fate

Are we really free? Don't these creation myths—from Middle-earth or from other texts like the Bible and the Bhagavad Gita—suggest that humans are in a sense "stuck" inside a universe that is far beyond our control? Does Ilúvatar or the Judeo-Christian-Islamic God, being all-powerful and all-knowing, having devised a "plan" for the world, imply that we do not have any freedom to exercise in daily life? Hasn't everything been determined in advance?

parable

A simple story that is intended to teach a lesson or moral.

Tolkien weaves these questions into his creation myths first with the "gifts" that Ilúvatar gives to men: the gift of free will that extends beyond their given situation, and the gift of death. These gifts detach human life from the fate of Middle-earth (the way that elves are connected to the world, and cannot leave it except through violence or despair). The lives of men are the fulcrum on which real freedom rests. This means that the stories of men, begun in the First Age but more carefully expressed in *Lord of the Rings*, are more political than stories about elves and dwarves. The politics of men are more fluid and changeable than those of the other races. In fact, the only other beings that seem capable of shifting back and forth from good to evil in quite the same way are beings of Power: the Valar and Maiar (e.g. Morgoth, Sauron, and Saruman).

The Fall

For Tolkien, all stories involve a fall from grace, a disruption of primal perfection, a conflict that must be confronted or resolved. "There cannot be any 'story' without a fall—all stories are ultimately about the fall—at least not for human minds as we know them and have them."[27] When he refers to "the fall," he is alluding to the Christian myth of the rebellion of Lucifer, who is cast out of Heaven and establishes his dominion in Hell. "The fall" can also allude to Adam and Eve being cast out of paradise, an analog to Lucifer's arrogance and independence. As easy as it might be to connect the Christian "fall" with Tolkien's cosmogony, he insists that his are "different in form ... to that of Christian myth. These tales are 'new,' they are not directly derived from other myths and legends, but they must inevitably contain a large measure of ancient wide-spread motives or elements."[28] Just as the gods fall away from union with Ilúvatar, the elves fall away from Valinor through their own rebellion, and men are similarly corrupted by Sauron's tempting influence into attacking Valinor directly, after which they are prohibited from sailing West. Tolkien argues:

> [T]he *Downfall* is partly the result of an inner weakness in Men—consequent, if you will, upon the first Fall, (unrecorded in these tales), repented but not finally healed. Reward on earth is more dangerous for men than punishment! The Fall is achieved by the cunning of Sauron in exploiting this weakness. Its central theme is (inevitably, I think, in a story of Men) a Ban, or Prohibition.[29]

THE HOBBIT

Tolkien had been composing children's literature for a number of years before he was inspired to write a story about a hobbit. Every December for decades, Tolkien would write and illustrate outlandish letters from Father Christmas (or Santa) to his children. These stories involved an expanding cast of characters, including snow elves, gnomes, cave bears, and Father Christmas's principle helper, a hapless polar bear.[1] It was in 1930, while teaching and researching at Pembroke College, Oxford, that he began crafting a tale about a hobbit, a little creature he invented that resembles a gnome or a dwarf. A hobbit is, in fact, a childlike adult, so it is relatable to children. *The Hobbit* won enormous critical and popular success; it has not been out of print since it was published in 1937, undergoing several important revisions in subsequent editions, being translated into dozens of languages, and adapted into movies, graphic novels, and video games.

The mere existence of *The Hobbit* may have been the launch pad for Tolkien's later success. After selling out run after run of *The Hobbit*, Tolkien's publishers clamored for more hobbit stories. But Tolkien had something else in mind: a larger, more complex story that would eventually become *The Lord of the Rings*. This would be years in the making. In order to fit *The Hobbit* into the ancient mythological creations that make up *The Silmarillion* and then into the wider conflict between light and dark in *The Lord of the Rings*, Tolkien made Bilbo's magic

When Tolkien published *The Hobbit* in 1937, it was intended as a children's book. While indeed popular with young readers, it also found an audience with many adults.

ring into the One Ring, the object around which the entire fate of the world revolves. Knowing how the One Ring affects the history of Middle-earth, hindsight adds extra weight and intensity to the events of *The Hobbit* without ruining what is at heart a lively, action-packed adventure story. Some might even prefer *The Hobbit* over *The Lord of the Rings*; as Harold Bloom puts it: "I suspect that *The Lord of the Rings* is fated to become only an intricate Period Piece, while *The Hobbit* may well survive as Children's Literature. Really good-natured fantasy is hard to come by, and one convincing personality at its center is all it requires."[2] That personality is Bilbo Baggins, the hero of the novel, the unassuming little creature full of potential.

The Plot of *The Hobbit*

The Hobbit, or There and Back Again, tells the story of Bilbo Baggins (a hobbit), Gandalf the Grey (a wizard), and a band of dwarves led by Thorin Oakenshield, who go on a quest to reclaim the Lonely Mountain, the ancestral home of the dwarves that had been conquered by a dragon, Smaug. The dragon had been attracted to the immense wealth the dwarves accumulated—now, centuries later, Smaug guards the treasure.

Bilbo is a reluctant but ultimately crucial member of the party; Gandalf convinces him to go on the quest, and he convinces the dwarves that Bilbo will be useful as "a burglar." Gandalf reveals his power and tactical intelligence early in the novel when he saves the party from becoming dinner for a trio of trolls. In another episode, chased this time by goblins, the party is separated in the tunnels below the Misty Mountains, and Bilbo finds himself alone with a strange, ghoulish creature named Gollum. Gollum has been living underground for centuries, guarding his "precious," a magical ring that makes

Bilbo Baggins (portrayed here by Martin Freeman in the film adaptation) is the unlikely hero of *The Hobbit*.

a person invisible when they wear it. (This ring turns out to be the One Ring, the ring of power that Sauron forged and imbued with all his evil power. The nature of the ring is not revealed—or, rather, invented—until *The Lord of the Rings* is published.) Bilbo stumbles on the ring and uses it to escape from Gollum. After finding his way back to the group, Bilbo, Gandalf, and the dwarves are attacked by the goblins, but are saved again, this time by giant eagles.

After run-ins with giant spiders in Mirkwood Forest and escaping the jails in the realm of the Woodelves, the group finally reaches the Lonely Mountain. Bilbo fulfills his role as "burglar" by sneaking into Smaug's lair, learning of his weakness, and stealing some of the treasure. Smaug sets out to destroy the nearby town, thinking they have mounted a plan of attack on his lair, but an archer in the town (having learned of the small point of vulnerability in Smaug's armor) kills him with a well-placed arrow. The dwarves take back the Lonely Mountain, but are seduced by the treasure, just as their ancestors were, and refuse to share it with the nearby town (destroyed by Smaug) and the wood elves, who are owed treasure from centuries before. Thorin in particular is adamant that he will never share the treasure. Bilbo tries to negotiate by giving the men and elves the Arkenstone, the most valuable piece of treasure, but Thorin only becomes more enraged. An army of dwarves appears to support Thorin in his defense of the treasure, but before a war breaks out between the three armies, Gandalf directs everyone's attention to the approaching army of goblins and wargs (dog-like monstrous creatures). The ensuing fighting became known as the Battle of the Five Armies. The giant eagles reappear and help the dwarves, elves, and men defeat the goblins and wargs. Thorin is killed and Bilbo returns to the Shire with a share of the treasure, making him the wealthiest hobbit in the land.

Themes

Greed and Generosity

Thorin Oakenshield is a typical dwarf in that he is totally overtaken by the splendor of the treasure hoard that is liberated from the dragon. Instead of living up to his royal heritage, Thorin is infected by greed and ends up losing his chance at heroism. Bilbo, on the other hand, represents a generous spirit: He declines to kill Gollum in the caves, instead sneaking away from him; he attempts to avert war by negotiating a fair settlement of treasure; he declines the full share of treasure at the end, opting instead for a smaller (but still significant) portion; and he generally displays extraordinary bravery and selflessness in the face of danger. In some ways, the quest is not really to obtain treasure or defeat a monster, but to gain an understanding of something greater than oneself. This is what Bilbo—and presumably the reader as well—takes home with him.

The "Real" Enemy

The Hobbit involves several layers of conflict—internal conflicts in the main characters, conflicts between "good" characters and "evil" beings, and conflicts among men, dwarves, and elves. At each level the "real" enemy is revealed and confronted. For instance, Bilbo is torn between the two parts of himself—the Tookish desire to go out into the world, and the Bagginsish desire to stay home and ignore the world. While we initially think that his difficulty is with the danger of adventure, what we come to understand is that his real enemy is indifference. In order to be a part of the world, Bilbo has to go out into it and face its dangers, yes, but more importantly, he has to care for others. Similarly, Smaug is the great external enemy, but after Smaug dies, his greed and selfishness continue on in Thorin Oakenshield. The "real" monster is greed, not the dragon. Finally, men and elves at first declare the dwarves their enemy, and war seems inevitable. But Gandalf reminds everyone of the real enemy: the goblins and wargs. At each level of conflict, what first appears to be the problem is shown to be secondary, and the root problem is revealed.

The Hero's Quest

At the end of the novel, Bilbo is "writing his memoirs—he thought of calling them 'There and Back Again, A hobbit's Holiday.'"[3] This out-and-back movement is both literal and symbolic, and it forms the core of what a hero's journey traditionally means. The classical hero is a figure that represents the

An engraving depicts Odysseus on a voyage. The Greek hero's epic journey serves as a model for the one undertaken in *The Hobbit*.

best of humanity, and resembles everyone, to some extent. For example, Odysseus from Homer's *Iliad* and *Odyssey* is a typical hero figure. In those epic tales, Odysseus goes off to war, has many adventures, and spends years struggling to come home. In the end, he makes it back to his kingdom at Ithaca, reunites with his wife, and exacts revenge on his enemies. The journey has made him older, certainly, but also wiser and more human.

The journey of Odysseus is the journey we all make from childhood (when we are thrown out into the world by our mothers), through adulthood (when we face difficulties, obstacles, and conflict) and finally to the wisdom of old and the peace of death. Of course, not all hero stories trace a life all the way from birth to death; most stories of this shape recount a single important adventure or experience. But the point is that stories that resemble this basic template—hero leaves home in search of goal, faces challenges in pursuit of goal, overcomes challenges, brings new knowledge back home—are very easy to find, both in the ancient and modern worlds. In this light, every story from Homer's epics to an episode of *The Simpsons* is part of the same tradition.

Important Characters

Bilbo Baggins, Hero and Burglar

Bilbo Baggins is the protagonist of the novel, although he is not the only important character. But it is via Bilbo's perspective that the reader sees the world, and his personal journey that matters most. He is a hobbit, a "very well-to-do hobbit,"[4] who lives in The Hill in a sleepy corner of Middle-earth known as the Shire. His chief characteristic, as a member of the Baggins family, was that he was very "respectable, not only because most of them [the Baggins] were very rich, but also because they never had any adventures or did anything unexpected."[5] He is, in brief, an agreeable little man who is content to stay at home and stay out of trouble.

Bilbo Baggins can be considered a typical hero figure, and it's written right into the subtitle: "there and back again." One of the first conflicts of the novel is Bilbo's reluctance to even engage with adventure, with the unknown, with what he calls "the Tookish" side of him, referring to the branch of his family tree populated by warriors and wanderers. He is "called" to action, like all heroes, and has a hard time accepting the quest:

> As [the dwarves] sang the hobbit felt the love of beautiful things made by hands and by cunning and by magic moving through him, a fierce and a jealous love, the desire of the hearts of dwarves. Then something Tookish woke up inside him, and he wished to go and see the great mountain, and hear the pine-trees and the water-falls, and explore the caves, and wear a sword instead of a walking-stick ... He shuddered; and very quickly he was plain Mr. Baggins of Bag-End, Under-Hill, again.[6]

This Tookish quality in Bilbo is what sends him out, but his Baggins half is what pulls him back home in the end. In fact, Bilbo continually struggles with these two parts of himself, especially at crucial moments on the journey. Later in the novel, when Bilbo is being asked to fulfill his role as "burglar," which is to say, to sneak into the dragon's lair and scout the situation, he faces his dual self once again:

> "Now you are in for it at last, Bilbo Baggins," he said to himself. "You went and put your foot right in it that night of the party, and now you have got to pull it out and pay for it! Dear me, what a fool I was and am!" said the least Tookish part of him. "I have absolutely no use for dragon-guarded treasures, and the whole lot could

stay here for ever, if only I could wake up and find this beastly tunnel was my own fronthall at home!"[7]

The argument between his two selves heightens the idea that the journey is a dream/nightmare, and that there are two realities at work.

Timothy O'Neill has interpreted Bilbo's journey as a kind of psychoanalytic allegory, or a symbolic story of facing one's dreams, nightmares, and deepest desires in order to come to terms with one's self. "Bilbo's world is a dream world, a Faërie world"[8] and the monsters and objects he encounters can be interpreted as expressions of his unconscious needs and wants. Gollum, whom Bilbo encounters in the caves (representing a descent into his unconscious, yet again), was not always the slimy creature he is; he used to be a hobbit. The meeting between Bilbo and Gollum sets in motion a series of events that alters the entire world; "symbolically this is the pivot point of the story, and the most powerful juxtaposition of forces."[9] Through this meeting, O'Neill argues, we can understand that Bilbo represents a Self that "has courageously (more or less) entered the forbidden recesses of the unconscious and collided unexpectedly with its dark mirror image. The collision is brief and incomplete ... The only possible end of this dream lies many years and many miles ahead, at the Cracks of Doom."[10] The notion of confronting a dark nightmare version of oneself is magnified in Bilbo's encounter with the dragon, which O'Neill reminds us is a typical symbolic animal in dreams and ancient mythological imagery. And in the end, what Bilbo wins is more "than golden chalices and glittering jewels; his treasure is the treasure of the Self, beside which the wealth of the King under the Mountain, the splendor and worldly pomp and lucre are small change."[11]

Gandalf is the wise and powerful wizard dedicated to fighting Sauron and his dark forces. Sir Ian McKellen played the character in both the *Hobbit* and *Lord of the Rings* trilogies.

Gandalf the Grey, the Guide, the Wizard

Harold Bloom calls Gandalf a "rude" and "self-important wizard,"[12] and in a way that is true, especially of Gandalf as he appears in *The Hobbit*. We have to remember that at this point in his work, Tolkien had not thought through the full scope and sequence of the epic to come, so Gandalf was allowed to be curmudgeonly and less-than-divine as he goes about leading the expedition to the Misty Mountains. Nonetheless, Gandalf is a force for good. He encourages Bilbo to join the quest for the treasure, and he saves the group a number of times along the way, including from the three stone trolls who are all set to eat them for dinner.

Gandalf fits the stereotype of "guide" or "teacher," which is a common role in epic and heroic fables. (Chiron the centaur, who tutors Hercules, is one such guide character from ancient Greek mythology; Yoda from the *Star Wars* series of films would qualify; Merlin in the Arthurian legends is yet another.) Gandalf's cleverness is both tactical—he understands the value of surprise in battle—as well as political—he arranges for the entire party, fifteen people, to arrive at the lodge of the "skin-changer" Beorn, a notorious recluse. "Mr. Baggins saw then how clever Gandalf had been. The interruptions had really made Beorn more interested in the story, and the story had kept him from sending the dwarves off at once like suspicious beggars."[13] His finest hours, though, come during the combination of political and military upheaval at the end of the novel in the Battle of the Five Armies. Gandalf, in the nick of time, saves Bilbo from being killed by Thorin in a murderous rage, then halts the armies of dwarves and elves bent on attacking each other, redirects their attention to the advancing goblin army, and then seems to play some part in summoning the eagles who turn the tide of the war. The Elvenking, on saying goodbye after the war is won, puts it succinctly: "Farewell! O Gandalf! May you ever appear where you are most needed and least expected!"[14]

Thorin Oakenshield

If you recall from the *Silmarillion* materials, dwarves are very old creatures who do not live forever as elves do, but nonetheless are blessed with extraordinarily long lifespans. They are elemental creatures, preferring to work in the dark underground than to spend time in forests aboveground. Like elves, they are master craftsmen who are particularly-

The dwarves get ready to embark on a quest to infiltrate the Lonely Mountain and reclaim the treasure guarded by Smaug.

good at forging weapons, armor, and jewelry. Because of their interest in mining, they are experts in all sorts of metal as well as gemstones. (Their involvement in the setting of a Silmaril into a piece of jewelry is what leads to their ancient feud with the elves.) They are the only race who are skilled enough to fashion a special metal, harder than any weapon, known as mithril. This material is exquisitely valuable; a single shirt of chainmail made from mithril is worth an entire fortune. (One of Bilbo's treasures, which he passes on to Frodo in the *Lord of the Rings*, is a mithril shirt.)

Thorin Oakenshield and his company of dwarves are on a mission to regain the Lonely Mountain, their ancestral home and stronghold, and the dwarven treasure contained in it. A century and a half before the quest, Smaug the dragon attacked the fortress and stole the treasure, destroying the nearby town of Dale and killing or running off all the dwarves in the mountain.

Thorin is an heir to the throne in the Lonely Mountain, and is a very imperial character: he uses his status to lord over his crew and to belittle Bilbo throughout the mission. When they finally kill Smaug, Thorin is obsessed with the treasure and the Arkenstone (the most valuable gem in the treasure horde) to the point that he is willing to kill Bilbo and deny the rightful claims of the Lake Town people and the elves to their share of the captured loot. He fights valiantly during the Battle of the Five Armies, and before he dies of his wounds he is able to apologize to Bilbo and try to redeem his earlier bad behavior.

Smaug

Tolkien's greedy, intelligent talking dragon, also known as Smaug the Magnificent, is a centuries old fire-drake. Like many dragons in mythology, Smaug flies, breathes fire, and is able to destroy entire towns. He is also extremely long lived. Tolkien's inspiration for this particular dragon seems to have been the dragon from *Beowulf* and the later thirteenth century dragon Fáfnir from the Icelandic *Volsunga Saga*. Tolkien, if you recall, was an expert in these myths and epics, and had a habit of deliberately re-creating (and making his own) charac-

"THE QUEST OF EREBOR": THE BRIDGE BETWEEN THE HOBBIT AND THE LORD OF THE RINGS

Why is Gandalf mixed up in a dwarf's quest for treasure? And why does he insist on involving Bilbo in the adventure? These central questions are not answered in *The Hobbit*, but they are important for linking the novel with the later adventures involving the Ring and the fight against Sauron. Tolkien does provide this bridge material in a story titled "The Quest of Erebor," posthumously published in *Unfinished Tales*. The narrator is Frodo, but the story consists mostly of Gandalf recounting how he came to join Thorin Oakenshield's quest. Gandalf was concerned that Smaug might become a powerful weapon or ally to Sauron, and so wanted to find a way to deal with him. At a chance meeting with Thorin at Bree, he learns that Thorin wants to confront the dragon as well (to reclaim his ancestral home and treasure). Gandalf agrees to help, and wonders how they can accomplish their task, when "Suddenly in my mind these three things came together: the great Dragon with his lust, and his keen hearing and scent; the sturdy heavy-booted dwarves with their old burning grudge; and the quick, soft-footed Hobbit, sick at heart (I guessed) for a sight of the wide world."[15] Thorin reluctantly agrees to the inclusion of a tiny, weak hobbit, and the rest is history.

ters and situations from older traditions. Scholars have argued persuasively for the connection between Tolkien and these earlier texts,[16] but it might be interesting to compare Smaug with the dragons from George R. R. Martin's fantasy novels *A Song of Ice and Fire*, remade for television as *Game of Thrones*. In this new and immensely popular fantasy world (that obviously takes some of its inspiration from Tolkien's storytelling), dragons are at the center of a political and military surge. But the dragons in *Ice and Fire* are nonverbal and for the most part treated as weapons rather than being individuated actors, like Smaug. This has the effect, it seems, of making dragons neither good nor evil, but something above the affairs of humans and other beasts. Tolkien's dragons are squarely evil.

Gollum and the Ring

Of all the events in *The Hobbit*, the one that has the most far-reaching consequences is Bilbo's encounter with the creature Gollum, and the finding of a magic ring. When Tolkien first composed this novel, the ring did not feature so prominently as it would after *The Lord of the Rings* was published. In hindsight, then, already knowing the arc of the entire epic, Bilbo's discovery of the magic ring is portentous. Making his way in the darkness under the mountain path, separated from his friends, Bilbo

> Crawled along for a good way, till suddenly his hand met what felt like a tiny ring of cold metal lying on the floor of the tunnel. It was a turning point in his career, but he did not know it. He put the ring in his pocket almost without thinking; certainly it did not seem of any particular use at the moment.[17]

Gollum is described in this novel as a "small slimy creature" and the narrator doesn't "know where he came from, nor who or what he was."[18] He lives by the underground lake, taking care of his "precious" (the ring) and killing the occasional goblin for dinner. Gollum's backstory is given in *The Lord of the Rings*, and we learn that he was once a hobbit himself, one of the riverfolk, and that he had transformed into the withered, reptilian creature through long possession of the One Ring, which had warped and twisted his mind. In fact, Gollum constantly talks to himself as if he is doubled, arguing and carrying on conversations with the other half of his mind. Just

Gollum is the strange creature who is responsible for Bilbo taking possession of the One Ring.

within the context of *The Hobbit*, Gollum and Bilbo function as mirror images: Bilbo, too, maintains an internal disagreement between his Baggins and Tookish nature. That Gollum goes on to play such a crucial role in *The Lord of the Rings* underscores his symbolic importance to Tolkien's project. The ring itself is of course the main problem of the entire epic, but everyone's ignorance of its real power—including the narrator's, Bilbo's, and Gollum's—makes the opening scenes of *The Lord of the Rings* more dramatically effective.

THE LORD OF THE RINGS

*T*he *Lord of the Rings* is Tolkien's magnum opus, a long, complex epic of the battle between good and evil, light and dark, destruction and creation, human and monster. It was written after the roaring success of *The Hobbit* at the insistence of Tolkien's publishers, who wanted to capitalize on the momentum of the earlier work. It is a logical question: Why not a sequel? The "sequel" to *The Hobbit* ended up becoming the main event, and besides selling more than 150 million copies, has taken its place on numerous "best of" lists since its publication in 1954. Tolkien wrote it as a single long work, but his publishers requested that it be released as a trilogy, the overarching title of which is *The Lord of the Rings*, and the individual books *The Fellowship of the Ring, The Two Towers,* and *The Return of the King.*

If we were to attempt to "explain" *The Lord of the Rings,* how would we begin? This is a daunting task, not least because the work is so varied in its content, characters, events, and themes. Luckily, Tolkien himself has commented on the book. In the foreword to the second edition, he writes:

> As for any inner meaning or 'message', it has in the intention of the author none. It is neither allegorical nor topical. As the story grew it put down roots (into the past) and threw out unexpected branches: but its

Tolkien wrote in 1955: "Nothing has astonished me more (and I think my publishers) than the welcome given to *The Lord of the Rings*. But it is, of course, a constant source of consolation and pleasure to me."

main theme was settled from the outset by the inevitable choice of the Ring as the link between it and *The Hobbit*.[1]

Tolkien is adamant that his novel does not covertly resemble World War II, which erupted just after he began writing, nor does it resemble his own experience as a soldier in World War I. This is not to say that we cannot interpret the stories, but only that Tolkien did not write them with a particular interpretation or meaning in mind. To make this point clear, he notes that there is a difference between applicability and allegory. "Applicability" refers to the ability of a reader to apply the events, themes, motifs, and images to his or her own life. Literary critics call this symptomatic meaning, which is the meaning that a reader's own circumstances bring to a work of art, quite apart from the intentions of the author. "Allegory," or a story that hides a political or moral message behind a symbolic arrangement of characters and settings, is something that an author imposes on the reader. "I cordially dislike allegory in all its manifestations," notes Tolkien in his characteristically diplomatic tone, "I much prefer history, true or feigned, with its varied applicability to the thought and experience of readers."[2]

What follows is an attempt to outline a few of the key themes, but following Tolkien's lead, it is important for each reader to encounter the text on their own terms and uncover their own meanings and feelings from the stories. Tolkien very much wanted readers to engage with his stories without trying to find a hidden key to unlock all the secrets and "solve" the text.

Plot

The Lord of the Rings is about the final confrontation between the forces of evil that have been plaguing Middle-earth since its creation millennia before. Ilúvatar (the One God) created the universe, but his most talented "angel" (or Ainur) Melkor rebels with his own plans, pitting harmony against dissonance. Melkor decides to take control of Ilúvatar's new creation, Middle-earth. At each step, what the forces of light have planned for Earth, Melkor (also known as Morgoth) perverts into something destructive and dark. Morgoth even infiltrates Valinor and undermines the peace there, going so far as to destroy the sacred Two Trees. After the struggle for control of the Silmarils, Morgoth is defeated, and he is imprisoned for eternity.

But Morgoth's lieutenant, a Maiar named Sauron, survives and bides his time. Eventually, he too infiltrates the peaceful kingdoms of Middle-earth, helping to create the Rings of Power and distribute them to elves, dwarves, and men. But secretly he forges the One Ring that controls all the others; he invests all his power into the Ring. Ultimately, a human king cuts off his finger and takes the ring for himself. But the problem with the One Ring is that it can't really be wielded except by Sauron, and it will corrupt the heart of any other bearer, making him cruel and selfish. Eventually Bilbo and then Frodo come into possession of the Ring.

When Gandalf learns that the Ring has been found, he sets in motion a mighty quest to infiltrate Sauron's strong-

> **allegory**
>
> A story that masks an underlying moral or political meaning.

> **motif**
>
> A repeating pattern, or a recurrent theme, character, or image in a work of literature

> **symptomatic meaning**
>
> Understanding a work of art based on current social conditions rather than the context of the work when it was created.

hold, Mordor, and throw the Ring back into the fires from which it was forged—the only way to really destroy it. While Frodo (and his friend Sam) sneak into Mordor with the Ring, Aragorn and the armies of men are resisting Sauron's military forces in a last ditch effort to regain control of Middle-earth. Aragorn is supposed to fulfill a prophecy about the return of the king of Gondor, and in the end, after defeating Sauron

Frodo Baggins (portrayed by Elijah Wood in the film trilogy) inherits Bilbo's ring in *The Fellowship of the Ring,* which leads to an epic journey similar to his cousin's years before.

and destroying the Ring, a new Age of Middle-earth begins in which men will rule and the elves sail back to Valinor in the West. Evil is vanquished and the good people of the world must rebuild and renew lands that have been scorched by the war that Sauron unleashed.

A Few Significant Characters

There are too many characters to list—the full text of the novels includes a massive index—and the wider Middle-earth fantasy world includes at least 982 characters (spanning *The Hobbit*, *The Lord of the Rings*, *The Silmarillion*, and the other texts), according to a fascinating statistical analysis of Tolkien's works called "The LOTR Project."[3] Of the central characters, only a handful are essential to illuminate the bigger themes of the text.

Frodo Baggins

Frodo is Bilbo's adopted "cousin" (but because of their age difference, Bilbo calls Frodo his nephew) and heir. Frodo has inherited the rings from Bilbo, and becomes the "ring bearer," the one whose task it is to carry the Ring to its destruction. He is the most important hero character in the novel. He is given the crucial, world-saving task; he is forced to leave home; he faces obstacles; and his journey comes to resemble a kind of metaphor for life, love, and sacrifice in everyday human existence. W. H. Auden, commenting on his friend Tolkien's achievements in fantasy storytelling, notes that there are two kinds of "Quest Hero": "One resembles the hero of Epic; his superior *arête* [excellence] is manifest to all." Odysseus, Jason who goes after the Golden Fleece, Beowulf, Hercules, and Achilles are all epic heroes in this sense. Their almost super-human talents, strength, and ingenuity are part of the reason for their quest in the first place. "The other type," explains Auden, "so common in fairy tales, is the hero whose *arête* is concealed. The youngest son, the weakest, the least clever, the one whom everybody would judge as least likely to succeed, turns out to be the hero when his manifest betters have failed."[4]

Auden's insight is perfectly in line with how Tolkien sees his project in creating Middle-earth: the important characters are those considered insignificant. As Gandalf (or, Mithrandir) notes in *The Silmarillion*, "Many are the strange chances of the world ... and help oft shall come from the hands of the weak when the Wise falter."[5] In addition, the idea of a hero who is not grand, popular, and noteworthy runs parallel to the idea that Tolkien's Christianity informs his tales even if it does not appear explicitly. From a literary perspective, Christ is a lowly son of a carpenter; he is born in a stable, where animals sleep; he is never wealthy, often unpopular, and yet becomes the ultimate heroic figure. So goes Frodo, the diminutive hobbit.

Gandalf

Gandalf the wizard comes as close to a Christ-like heroism as any other character besides Frodo. Gandalf, like Christ, has the added distinction of having been resurrected from death (after his fight with the Balrog, during which he sacrifices himself for his friends—another Christ-like attribute). Like Frodo and Christ, Gandalf is much more than he seems and deliberately maintains an unassuming outward appearance. His role is more guide than hero, however, since he supports the main actor's projects and helps direct their goals. Gandalf does fight effectively with his wizard staff as well as his sword Glamdring (an ancient elvish weapon that he finds during *The Hobbit*). Gandalf is also associated with Shadowfax, the

WIZARDS OF MIDDLE-EARTH

Gandalf the Grey is one of the most memorable characters in literature and film, but he is not the only wizard in Middle-earth. According to Tolkien's materials, both the major texts and the minor, posthumously published sketches, there were five wizards in Middle-earth, known as the Istari. They are Maiar spirits in human form, sent across the sea to Middle-earth to fight Sauron.

Gandalf the Grey (who subsequently dies and is reborn as Gandalf the White) is considered the wisest of the five wizards.

Radagast the Brown is a squirrelly wizard whose main interest is the beasts and plants of the Earth; at times this focus aligns him with Gandalf, who works to help men and elves.

Saruman the White was originally the leader of the White Council, a group of powerful beings dedicated to stopping Sauron. After studying the dark lord and the history of the rings, however, Saruman became convinced that he could overthrow Sauron after aligning with him, thus gaining the One Ring for himself. (He raises an army at his stronghold Isengard, but is defeated by the ents.)

The other two wizards are almost ignored by Tolkien's material. The only thing we know is that they are known as the blue wizards, and they were given a mission to the East, to rally support or organize resistance against Mordor. Otherwise, few details exist about these characters.

Aragorn is a Ranger of the North, a brave warrior who is charged with protecting the Shire, where people call him Strider. He is portrayed by Viggo Mortensen in the film adaptations.

greatest of the horses of Middle-earth, who only allows the wizard to ride him.

Aragorn

Also known as Strider, Aragorn is the descendant of the ancient kings of men and is directly related to Isildur, the last man to have faced Sauron in battle (and who cut the One Ring from Sauron's hand). He

allusion
An indirect reference.

is also a heroic figure in the novels—there are many—but for yet different reasons. Aragorn reluctantly accepts his destiny as a ruler over others—thus proving his worthiness for such a job—and performs countless selfless acts of bravery, in the mold of the self-sacrificing Christ figure. Aragorn is also the "resurrected king" figure, which is another indirect allusion to the return of the Christian messiah. While this all fits neatly into a Christian framework, true to Tolkien's intentional disconnect between fairy tales and explicit religious doctrine, the death and resurrection of the king is a common motif in mythological and folk tale sources. (For a fantastically detailed early anthropological and comparative account of this motif, see Sir James Frazer's monumental book *The Golden Bough*.[6])

Elrond

Also referred to as Elrond Half-Elven, this lord of the elves in Rivendel is an ancient being, having been born in the First Age, thousands of years before the appearance of hobbits and men. Because of his extreme age, he is wisdom and knowledge incarnate: He seems to *know things*, even sensing the future. Tolkien commented on what he wanted to express with Elrond's character:

Elrond symbolises throughout the ancient wisdom, and his House represents Lore—the preservation in reverent memory of all tradition concerning the good, wise, and beautiful. It is not a scene of *action* but of *reflection*. Thus it is a place visited on the way to all deeds, or 'adventures'. It may prove to be on the direct road (as in *The Hobbit*); but it may be necessary to go from there in a totally unexpected course. So necessarily in *The Lord of the Rings*, having escaped to Elrond from the imminent pursuit of present evil, the hero departs in a wholly new direction: to go and face it at its source.[7]

Elrond is a kind of gatekeeper and assists in all kinds of navigational and strategic situations, from launching the Fellowship to helping Gandalf and the dwarves interpret their treasure map. In the end of *The Lord of the Rings*, Elrond is also present as the elves, along with Gandalf, Frodo, Bilbo, and a handful of others, sail into the West toward the "Undying Lands." Elrond, then, shepherds even the transition between the age of elves (the Third Age) and the age of men (the Fourth Age).

Themes

The Problem with Evil

It might be too simplistic to say that *The Lord of the Rings* is a battle between good and evil, since that reduces what are enormously complex ambiguities. Is Frodo all good, Gollum all evil? This is a real problem in the text, since Frodo has internalized parts of the Ring's destructive power, and Gollum is awakened to his former peaceful self. Or another question: Is the desire to do good the first step to doing evil? Desire, it seems, has a kind of corruption built into it. Gandalf in Peter Jackson's film *The Fellowship of the Ring* highlights this tension when he declares that Frodo should not offer him the Ring: "Don't tempt me Frodo! I dare not take it, not even to keep it safe. Understand, Frodo, I would use this ring from a desire to do good, but through me it would wield a power too great and terrible to imagine."[8] Therefore, evil is an internal problem—Sauron is just the external representation of evil. Frodo's quest ultimately becomes an internal journey to defeat his own desires and feelings.

One could compare this kind of internal struggle that Frodo faces with the same theme in the *Star Wars* films by George Lukas. Anakin Skywalker is led down the path to the Dark Side—and to his becoming Darth Vader—when he allows himself to fall in love. As his teacher Yoda (a counterpart to Gandalf) explains: Love for an individual leads to fear of losing them; fear leads to anger; anger leads to hate; and hate leads to the Dark Side. Goodness and Evil are bound together.

The Diminishing Scale of Mythology

The scale of Tolkien's mythologies diminishes over time: "The Music of the Ainur" concerns Ilúvatar and the other "gods," cosmic forces of creation, harmony, and dissonance. *The Silmarillion* narrates how those cosmic beings "descended" to Earth and waged a war, where the metaphorical harmony and dissonance are translated into an actual fight between the Valar and Morgoth, with troops and strongholds and so on. The main actors in those tales are great and powerful beings: Maiar, elves, potent men. When we finally enter the story in the Third Age, the great powers are reduced. Morgoth has been replaced by his lieutenant Sauron. The great Valar are now physically manifested Maiar like Gandalf and Saruman. The main actors are more "ordinary" beings like hobbits, men

MEN AND WOMEN IN *THE LORD OF THE RINGS*

There's no way around it: *The Lord of the Rings* is a story dominated by men and the male perspective. According to the statistical analysis at LOTR Project, 82 percent of the characters in Tolkien's body of work are male. Of the 472 human characters mentioned, just 62 are female. Only a single dwarf female is mentioned by name—Dís—and then only because her two sons bravely defend Thorin during the Battle of the Five Armies.[9] There are only a handful of candidates for significant female characters in all of Tolkien. One is Arwen, an elf princess who is in love with Aragorn and who gives up her immortality to be with him. And while Arwen is justifiably powerful as an elf, she ends up finding her true calling in domestic bliss, married to Aragorn.

A similar downward trend can be seen with the other major candidate for female power: Éowyn, a human, shieldmaiden of Rohan, who also falls in love with Aragorn. After her amazing performance on the battlefield (she disguises herself as a man so she can fight) against Sauron's forces and her legendary killing of the Nazgul Witch King, Éowyn fades fast. As Faramir gazes at her and asks her if she loves him, "the heart of Éowyn changed" and she declares, "I will be a shieldmaiden no longer, nor vie with the great Riders—I will be a healer, and love all things that grow and are not barren."[10] She jokes that Faramir will have "tamed" her; they laugh about that, and then kiss, sealing their new roles as Steward of Gondor and Wife of Steward of Gondor. Éowyn's power to act disappears.

Is this entire project built on a kind of sexism, on the assumption that men are actors and women are passive, more important to be seen and not heard? It is a product of its era, to be sure, and these sexist assumptions are commonplace even in the twenty-first century.

like Aragorn and Boromir, and elves like Legolas. Finally, after helping to win the War of the Ring, the elves depart entirely; men replace elves. The "magic" of the elves sails with them over the sea to the West.

This gradual "reduction" in scale can be seen in other mythological systems. For example, in Greek myth, the story of violence among family members is passed down from the great cosmic gods to the epic characters in Homer's poems to the more mundane kings and queens of recorded history and finally to our own lives.

Frodo receives a kiss from Galadriel, a royal elf, and one of few female characters in Tolkien's writings.

The Shire as Idyllic Home

Frodo, Sam, Merry, and Pippin are from the Shire, an out-of-the-way countryside with farmland, rolling hills, and burbling brooks. It is a vision of home as "natural," an idyllic rural space that is elevated to the level of metaphorical paradise. The Shire contains all the elements of a good life: fresh air, community, rich harvests, and excellent tobacco. For Frodo, the Shire embodies the concept of home: "I feel," Frodo says to Gandalf early in the saga, "that as long as the Shire lies behind, safe and comfortable, I shall find wandering more bearable: I shall

For Bilbo, Frodo, and the rest of the hobbits, the Shire represents home and safety. It stands in stark contrast to the perils and challenges the heroes face on their long journey.

know that somewhere there is a firm foothold, even if my feet cannot stand there again."[11] The saga begins in the Shire, with Bilbo's 111th birthday party, and ultimately, in one of the final chapters called "The Scouring of the Shire," when the hobbits return from their quest, they must restore peace and order by arresting and killing some bad characters who have taken over in their absence. Thus the arc of the novel is bracketed by the disruption and restoration of this paradise. Tolkien admits that his vision of the Shire is influenced by his early childhood in Sarehole, Birmingham, England.

Interestingly, this aspect of the stories is completely omitted from Peter Jackson's film adaptations of the novels. The Shire is only ever a place of harmony and natural beauty; in the film Wormtongue does kill Saruman, but the murder takes place on top of the Tower of Isengard after the battle, rather than in the Shire after being confronted by the hobbits. (For more on the challenges of adaptation, see chapter 5.) This effects a shift in emphasis from the restoration of paradise to the fulfillment of a political quest. The end of the *Lord of the Rings* films lean heavily on Aragorn regaining his throne, and then the ring bearers and elves departing for the Undying Lands. The part about reclaiming the Shire is ignored. But there are dramatic reasons for cutting the Battle of Bywater: in a film, it would destroy the emotional climax of defeating Sauron and destroying the Ring. Because films rely on narrative flow and clear emotional arcs—especially films like this, with "Hollywood"-style conflict/resolution structures—including any material extraneous to that story can kill it dead. As Gabriel Ruzin rightly points out

> In print, the battle cleverly shows that, even though the war has been won, evil will forever search for a foothold, even in realms thought untouchable. In other words,

89

Sauron is defeated but the world is still a dangerous place. In novel form, that works. On screen and for casual fans, there is no way to portray that without it being a hollow anticlimax.[12]

On the other hand, the dictates of cinematic storytelling can alter the tone and moral of the story, as we've already seen. What Ruzin sees as necessary to adaptation clearly erases (or at least diminishes) the sense that "evil will forever search for a foothold," one of the crucial messages of Tolkien's original.

"Leaf by Niggle," Minor Works, and Adaptations

Tolkien was a fantastically prolific writer, both of fiction and nonfiction. We have briefly examined his major works, but many smaller and less well-known texts remain. Several were published in Tolkien's lifetime, and most were edited and published posthumously by his son Christopher. *The Book of Lost Tales* was published in 1983 and 1984, in two parts, almost a decade after Tolkien's death. These volumes contain early drafts, and in some cases far more complex versions, of the mythologies that would eventually be transformed in *The Silmarillion*. They also show how invested Tolkien was in developing the mythological, as opposed to the novelistic or modern fictional narrative, aspects of Middle-earth. (Recall, *The Hobbit* was not originally intended to be the foundation for a saga, and *The Lord of the Rings* was only produced because of the success of *The Hobbit*.)

"Leaf by Niggle" is a short story Tolkien actually published, along with his essay "On Fairy-Stories," in a small book called *Tree and Leaf*. It is unconnected to Middle-earth lore, but it contains Tolkien's ideas about art and creation and so is helpful for a fuller understanding of his philosophy of fantasy. It also shadows the epics of Bilbo and Frodo in interesting ways. For example, the opening ought to make us think of the famous hobbits: "There was once a little man called Niggle, who had a long journey to make. He did not want to go, indeed the whole idea was distasteful to him; but he could not get out of

In 1972, Tolkien was awarded an honorary doctorate of letters from Oxford University, one of many honors conferred upon him toward the end of his life.

it."[1] Niggle is an artist who paints landscape scenes (and takes incredible pains with details like individual leaves). Instead of finishing his masterpiece, Niggle is always being called away to do something, usually a favor, often for his neighbor Parish. He keeps getting distracted. Finally, he's called away on his journey—we don't know where—and it turns out he's being sent to a kind of workhouse or forced labor. At the end of his time there, he's passed on to the "next stage" where his art is waiting for him in real life: He's being given a place in the country surrounded by his trees and forests and mountains. He and Parish enjoy the countryside, until Niggle travels out into the forest and eventually the mountain range that was only ever a hazy background in his paintings. His original painting, back home, crumbles, but a single leaf remains intact, and it's framed in a museum.

The tale is reminiscent of the stories of German writer Franz Kafka in the sense that it feels like a parable, and many administrative and logistical events happen to Niggle without his full knowledge or consent—he is moved from here to there, given these tasks or duties, told when to move on, etc. (Being caught up in a bureaucratic nightmare is typically Kafkaesque.) But it has a happy outcome (in contrast to Kafka, whose stories almost always end in tragedy or death), and as it progresses the story is unmistakably allegorical: it represents a kind of death (the unwanted journey, unfinished business), and travel to purgatory (a place where souls wait to be judged fit for heaven or hell), and finally his journey into paradise. Niggle, in being able to inhabit the "real" version of his painting, represents the artist who, like the elves in Middle-earth, create art for its own sake and not to dominate others. Niggle is so humble that he spends most of his time helping other people and not as much as he'd like working on his own projects. His reward is to enjoy the fulfillment of his vision after death.

The other major collection of Tolkien's fiction was published as *The History of Middle-Earth* in twelve volumes by Christopher Tolkien, from 1983 to 1996. It is a history of the development of the Middle-earth stories, told through the various drafts, early and late versions, letters to friends, and comparative analysis by Christopher Tolkien. These texts go into remarkable depth on the languages of Middle-earth, the complex histories of the major characters, even an etymological dictionary of the elvish tongues. (Tolkien was nothing if not thorough.) Reading *The History* emphasizes the magnitude of Tolkien's achievement as a creator: the sheer size of his effort, the breadth of his imagination, and the love and dedication with which he approached his work. No matter what literary critics say about the "quality" of his fiction, Tolkien has made an indelible mark on the world and the imaginations of so many readers.

The Films

We cannot end a discussion of the works of Tolkien without a word on how the major works have been adapted to other media. *The Hobbit* and *The Lord of the Rings* have both been made into films at various times, as well as graphic novels, games, and radio and stage dramatizations. *The Hobbit* was produced as an animated feature-length film by Rankin/ Bass Productions that was nominated for numerous awards when it came out in 1977. Director Ralph Bakshi produced an animated adaptation of the first half of *The Lord of the Rings* in 1978 that was a financial success and introduced cutting-edge animation and sound technologies (for the time), but he was never able to adapt the entire story. Rankin/Bass eventually

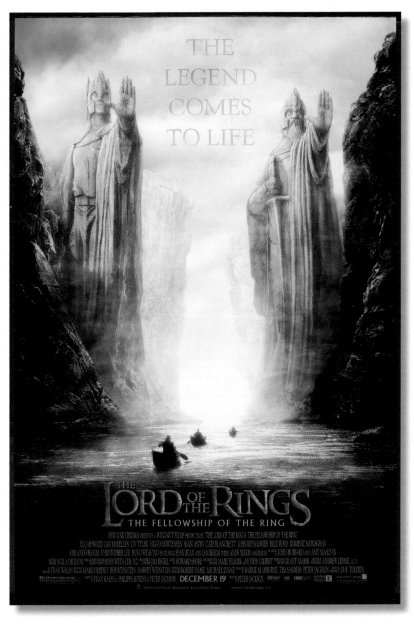

Although Tolkien was critical of efforts to turn his stories into film during his lifetime, Peter Jackson's blockbuster movies have at the very least brought the late writer's work to the attention of a new generation of readers. Sales of his books increased dramatically following the release of each film.

made a version of *Return of the King*, but it was not connected to the Bakshi film.

In 2001 director Peter Jackson released the first of six films based on Tolkien's work, *Lord of the Rings: The Fellowship of the Ring*. *The Two Towers* followed in 2002, and in 2003 Jackson released *The Return of the King*, completing the trilogy. He also made three feature-length films based on *The Hobbit*, which came out between 2012 and 2014. These films have been massively successful; each of the *Lord of the Rings* films cost approximately $94 million to produce and grossed between $800 million and $1.1 billion worldwide in box office sales alone. Each of the three *Hobbit* films also grossed around $1 billion.

As adaptations go, the Peter Jackson films are remarkably faithful to the source material. But Tolkien's books are so long and layered with context and history that editorial choices had to be made, while a few additions were included. The difficulty for Jackson and his production team was how the "Tolkien community" would react; the films are wonderful and exciting as pure entertainment, but for the large and active network of true fans, the films would either ruin or enhance a deeply felt story. In the end the films were well-received all around, with the bonus of financial success and awards.

One of the most interesting changes was the addition of the character Tauriel to *The Hobbit* films. Tauriel is depicted as the head of the Mirkwood elven guard; she is a talented fighter and excellent with a bow and arrow; and she is heroic and faithful. Introducing a new female character with such a strong role would seem like a positive, since it would be impossible to miss the fact that Tolkien's original stories are entirely driven by males. But Jackson and his writers have Tauriel motivated by love for one of the dwarves and pursued by Legolas, hence defined by a love triangle rather than by her own heroic quest or goal. But this is the challenge of adaptation in general, especially of works of literature that have dated or that are moralistic, like Tolkien's novels. How the adaptation is received will depend largely on current social conditions and questions. Race, class, gender, and politics are intensely contested in today's social climate. Audiences are much more critical of how women are represented on screen, how racial markings are used by filmmakers, and how power dynamics flow between and among characters. In an era when Spiderman will be portrayed by a young black actor, or Thor will be a woman, or the Black Panther stories will resonate with racial tensions in the United States, the question of how to adapt a book to a film suddenly has real-life consequences.

CHRONOLOGY

1892—Tolkien is born on January 3 in Bloemfontein, Orange Free State in South Africa.

1895—Travels to England with brother and mother in April. Tolkien's father contracts rheumatic fever in November; dies on February 15, 1896.

1904—Tolkien's mother is diagnosed with diabetes and dies.

1908—Tolkien meets future wife Edith Bratt.

1914—Becomes engaged to Edith.

1915—Trains as an officer; begins writing poetry.

1916—Tolkien and Edith are married on March 22.

1917—Writes *The Book of Lost Tales* (early version of *The ilmarillion*).

1918—Joins the staff of *The Oxford English Dictionary*.

1922—Begins work on *Sir Gawain and the Green Knight* with E. V. Gordon.

1924—Becomes a professor of English Language at Leeds University.

1925—Elected Rawlinson and Bosworth Professor of Anglo-Saxon at Oxford University.

1926—Becomes friends with C. S. Lewis; they form The Coalbiters, a literary group which will later become the Inklings.

1930—Begins work on *The Hobbit*.

1936—Lectures on "*Beowulf*: The Monsters and the Critics"; finishes *The Hobbit*.

1937—Begins work on *The Lord of the Rings*.

1939—Gives "On Fairy Stories" lecture.

1949—Finishes *The Lord of the Rings*.

1954—*The Fellowship of the Ring* and *The Two Towers* are published by Allen and Unwin.

1955—*The Return of the King* is published.

1959—Tolkien retires from Oxford.

1962—*The Adventures of Tom Bombadil* is published.

1964—*Tree and Leaf* is published.

1967—*Smith of Wooten Major* is published.

1971—Edith dies.

1973—Tolkien falls sick and dies on September 2.

1977—*The Silmarillion* is published.

1983–1996—Christopher Tolkien releases *The History of Middle-Earth* in twelve volumes, collecting a massive trove of drafts, variations, and unpublished stories relating to Tolkien's fantasy world.

1997—BBC Channel 4 and Waterstone's Bookstore reader poll lists *The Lord of the Rings* as the greatest book of the twentieth century

2001—*The Fellowship of the Ring* film is released (nominated for thirteen Oscars, wins four).

2002—*The Two Towers* film is released (nominated for six Oscars, wins two).

2003—*The Return of the King* film is released (wins eleven Oscars).

2012—*The Hobbit: An Unexpected Journey* film is released.

2013—*The Hobbit: The Desolation of Smaug* film is released.

2014—*The Hobbit: The Battle of the Five Armies* film is released.

CHAPTER NOTES

Introduction: Literary Roots

1. J. R. R. Tolkien, Christopher Tolkien, and Humphrey Carpenter, *The Letters of J.R.R. Tolkien*, 1st edition (Boston: Mariner Books, 2000), 288.
2. J. R. R. Tolkien, *The Two Towers: Being the Second Part of The Lord of the Rings* (Boston: Houghton Mifflin Harcourt, 2012), 38.
3. T. A. Shippey, *The Road to Middle-Earth: [How J.R.R. Tolken Created a New Mythology]*, rev. ed. (Boston: Houghton Mifflin Co, 2003), 2.
4. Joseph Pearce, *Tolkien: Man and Myth: A Literary Life*, 1st ed. (San Francisco: Ignatius PR, 1999), 2.
5. Andrew Rissik, "Guardian Review: JRR Tolkien by Tom Shippey," *Guardian*, September 1, 2000, http://www.theguardian.com/books/2000/sep/02/jrrtolkien.classics.
6. Harold Bloom, ed., *J.R.R. Tolkien's the Lord of the Rings*, Modern Critical Interpretations (Philadelphia: Chelsea House Publishers, 2000), 1.
7. Ibid.
8. Ibid., 2.
9. Ursula K. Le Guin, "The Child and the Shadow," *The Quarterly Journal of the Library of Congress* 32, no. 2 (1975): 141.
10. Bloom, *J.R.R. Tolkien's the Lord of the Rings*, 2.

Chapter 1. A Life of Fairy-Stories

1. Peter Gilliver, Jeremy Marshall, and Edmund Weiner, *The Ring of Words: Tolkien and the Oxford English Dictionary*, 1st ed. (Oxford University Press, 2009), 4.
2. Ibid., 6.

3. "History of the OED," *Oxford English Dictionary*, accessed May 5, 2016, http://public.oed.com/history-of-the-oed/.

4. "About the Inklings," *Mythopoeic Society*, accessed May 12, 2016, http://www.mythsoc.org/inklings/.

5. J.R.R. Tolkien, "On Fairy-Stories," in *The Monsters and the Critics and Other Essays*, ed. Christopher Tolkien (London: George Allen and Unwin, 1983), 111.

6. Ibid., 113.

7. Ibid.

8. Ibid., 114.

9. Tolkien, *The Two Towers*, 462.

10. Matthew T. Dickerson and Jonathan D. Evans, *Ents, Elves, and Eriador: The Environmental Vision of J.R.R. Tolkien* (Lexington, KY: University Press of Kentucky, 2006), xx.

11. Ibid., 242.

12. Kirill Yeskov, *The Last Ringbearer*, trans. Yisroel Markov, 2011, 11, http://ymarkov.livejournal.com/280578.html.

13. J. R. R Tolkien and Christopher Tolkien, *The Silmarillion*, 2001. xiii.

14. Ibid., xiii–xiv.

Chapter 2. *The Silmarillion*

1. J. R. R Tolkien and Christopher Tolkien, *The Silmarillion* (Boston: Houghton Mifflin, 2001), vii.

2. Ibid.

3. Alison Flood, "Guy Gavriel Kay: 'I Learned a Lot about False Starts from JRR Tolkien,'" *Guardian*, October 29, 2014, http://www.theguardian.com/books/2014/oct/29/guy-gavriel-kay-jrr-tolkien-interview-fionovar-tapesty-the-summer-tree.

4. Randel Helms, *Tolkien and the Silmarils* (Boston: Houghton Mifflin, 1981), 93.

5. Ibid., 94.

6. Tolkien and Tolkien, *The Silmarillion*, 15.

7. Ibid., 16.

8. Ibid., 30.

9. Ibid., 38.

10. Ibid., 39.

11. Ibid., 41.

12. Ibid., 42.

13. Ibid.

14. Ibid., 103.

15. Ibid., 104.

16. Ibid., 105.

17. Ibid., 43.

18. Ibid., 44.

19. Humphrey Carpenter, *J.R.R. Tolkien: A Biography*, ed. J. R. R. Tolkien, 1st ed. (Boston: Houghton Mifflin Company, 2000), 67–69.

20. Ibid., 105.

21. Tolkien and Tolkien, *The Silmarillion*, xi.

22. Ibid.

23. Ibid.

24. Ibid, xii.

25. Ibid.

26. Ibid. xvii.

27. Ibid., xv.

28. Ibid.

29. Ibid., xxi.

Chapter 3. *The Hobbit*

1. J. R. R. Tolkien, *Letters From Father Christmas*, rev. ed. (Boston: Mariner Books, 2004).

2. Harold Bloom, ed., *J.R.R. Tolkien*, Modern Critical Views (Philadelphia: Chelsea House Publishers, 2000), 2.

3. J. R. R. Tolkien, *The Hobbit, Or, There and Back Again*, 1st Mariner Books ed., 75th anniversary ed. (Boston: Houghton Mifflin Harcourt, 2012), 275.

4. Ibid., 3.

5. Ibid.

6. Ibid., 16.

7. Ibid., 197.

8. Timothy R. O'Neill, "The Individuated Hobbit," in *J.R.R. Tolkien*, ed. Harold Bloom, Modern Critical Views (Philadelphia: Chelsea House Publishers, 2000), 84.

9. Ibid., 86.

10. Ibid.

11. Ibid., 92.

12. Bloom, *J.R.R. Tolkien*, 2.

13. Tolkien, *The Hobbit, Or, There and Back Again*, 116.

14. Ibid., 267.

15. J. R. R. Tolkien, *Unfinished Tales of Númenor and Middle-Earth*, ed. Christopher Tolkien, Reissue edition (New York: Mariner Books, 2014), 337.

16. Jonathan Evans, "The Dragon-Lore of Middle-Earth: Tolkien and Old English and Old Norse Tradition," in *J.R.R. Tolkien and His Literary Resonances: Views of Middle-Earth* (Greenwood Publishing Group, 2000), 25–28.

17. Tolkien, *The Hobbit, Or, There and Back Again*, 65.

18. Ibid., 68.

Chapter 4. *The Lord of the Rings*

1. J. R. R. Tolkien, *The Lord of the Rings* (Boston: Mariner Books, 1999), xxiii.

2. Ibid, xxiv.

3. "Middle-Earth in Numbers - LotrProject," accessed May 10, 2016, http://lotrproject.com/statistics/.

4. W. H. Auden, "The Quest Hero," in *Tolkien and the Critics; Essays on J. R. R. Tolkien's the Lord of the Rings* (Notre Dame; London: University of Notre Dame Press, 1968), 46.

5. Tolkien and Tolkien, *The Silmarillion*, 361–362.

6. Sir James George Frazer, *The Golden Bough*, Abridged edition (Mineola, NY: Dover Publications, 2002).

7. Tolkien and Tolkien, *The Silmarillion*, xx.

8. Peter Jackson, *The Lord of the Rings: The Fellowship of the Ring*, Adventure, Drama, Fantasy, (2001).

9. "Middle-Earth in Numbers - LotrProject."

10. J. R. R. Tolkien, *The Return of the King: Being the Third Part of the Lord of the Rings*, Reissue edition (Boston: Mariner Books, 2012), 262.

11. Ibid., 68.

12. Gabriel Ruzin, "A Purist's Defense of Peter Jackson's Lord of the Rings Screenplay," *Shadowlocked*, December 13, 2010, http://www.shadowlocked.com/201012131120/opinion-features/a-purists-defense-of-peter-jacksons-lord-of-the-rings-screenplay.html.

Chapter 5. "Leaf by Niggle," Minor Works, and Adaptations

1. J. R. R. Tolkien, *Tree and Leaf: Including "Mythopoeia"* (London: HarperCollins Publishers Ltd, 2001), 100.

Literary Terms

allegory—A story that masks an underlying moral or political meaning.

allusion—An indirect reference.

apologist—One who defends something or someone in writing or speech.

canon—In literature, a list of works that have been deemed to be the most important of their time.

cosmogony—A cosmic creation theory or story, for example, the first chapter of the Book of Genesis.

dichotomy—A contrast between two things that are assumed to be separate or opposite.

epic—One of the oldest narrative genres, originally a long poem depicting a heroic quest, now simply refers to long works with heroes (not necessarily poems).

etymological—Having to do with the origins of a word.

lexicon—The vocabulary of a language.

moralistic—Emphasizing moral lessons or teachings.

motif—A repeating pattern, or a recurrent theme, character, or image in a work of literature.

parable—A simple story that is intended to teach a lesson or moral.

philology—The study of the history of language.

reductionism—The act of breaking down a complex idea into a very simple form.

symptomatic meaning—Understanding a work of art based on current social conditions rather than the context of the work when it was created.

tendentious—Promoting a particular cause or (usually controversial) point of view.

Major Works by
J. R. R. Tolkien

Sir Gawain and the Green Knight (1925)
The Hobbit, or There and Back Again (1937)
Beowulf: The Monsters and the Critics (1937)
Sir Orfeo (1944)
On Fairy-Stories (1947)
The Fellowship of the Ring (Lord of the Rings, vol. 1, 1954)
The Two Towers (Lord of the Rings, vol. 2, 1954)
The Return of the King (Lord of the Rings, vol. 3, 1955)
*The Adventures of Tom Bombadil and Other Verses from the Red
   Book* (1962)
Tree and Leaf ("On Fairy-Stories" and "Leaf by Niggle" in book
   form, 1964)

Posthumous Publications

*Translations of Sir Gawain and the Green Knight, Pearl and Sir
   Orfeo* (1975)
The Father Christmas Letters (1976)
The Silmarillion (1977)
Unfinished Tales of Númenor and Middle-earth (1980)
The Letters of J. R. R. Tolkien (1981)
The History of Middle-earth (12 volumes, 1983–1996)
The Children of Húrin (2007)
Beowulf: A Translation and Commentary (2014)
The Story of Kullervo (2015)

Further Reading

Books

Carpenter, Humphrey. *J. R. R. Tolkien: A Biography*. Boston, MA: Houghton Mifflin, 2000.

Day, David. *An Atlas of Tolkien*. San Diego, CA: Thunder Bay Press, 2015.

Fonstad, Karen Wynn. *The Atlas of Middle-Earth*. Boston, MA: Houghton Mifflin, 1991.

Kreeft, Peter. *The Philosophy of Tolkien: The Worldview Behind* The Lord of the Rings. San Francisco, CA: Ignatius Press, 2005.

Pearce, Joseph. *Tolkien: Man and Myth, a Literary Life*. San Francisco, CA: Ignatius Press, 2001.

Tyler, J. E. A. *The Complete Tolkien Companion*. New York, NY: St. Martin's Griffin, 2012.

Websites

One Wiki to Rule Them All
lotr.wikia.com/wiki/Main_Page
A Tolkien-specific wiki with wonderfully deep warehouses of information on everything from the books to adaptations and other Tolkien-related material.

The One Ring: The Home of Tolkien Online
www.theonering.com
Includes a vibrant community forum and more links, news, and Tolkien information.

The Tolkien Estate
www.tolkienestate.com
Contains in-depth information on everything from Tolkien's writing to his various invented language systems and links to art, books, and other related sites.

The Tolkien Society

www.tolkiensociety.org

An international association of Tolkien enthusiasts and scholars; this society was presided over by Tolkien himself. Tolkien's daughter is the current leader. It holds events, conferences, and other gatherings and has a Tolkien archive.

INDEX